Red Hair, Blue Lips

ISBN: 979-8-33609494-7

Published by OZ Creative Co. LLC. Edited and designed by Orli Zuravicky

Printed by Kindle Direct Publishing. First printing edition 2024.

Author photo by Alexandrea Tombrakos Weiss.

Some names have been changed to protect privacy.

Red Hair, Blue Lips

by Claire Harris Tunick

Contents

Preface

This memoir was born in an unairconditioned classroom at Columbia University's Teachers College during the summer of 1986. I was enrolled in a three-week, five- day-a-week, intensive workshop to learn the Writing Process: a method of teaching writing that was developed by Lucy Caulkins. Each morning was spent with a Caulkins-trained instructor on the skills necessary to teach the process of writing, which included planning, drafting, sharing, evaluating, revising, editing and publishing. Each afternoon, we students applied those skills to our own writing in a workshop guided by a published writer or poet. The writing process is based on the idea that students learn to write best when they write frequently, for extended periods of time, and on topics of their own choosing. So, in the afternoon after an hour of discussion, we began our own piece of writing that we would use to apply our newly learned skills.

I had difficulty coming up with a topic. We were taught that as instructors, if that were to occur in our classroom, we should have our students brainstorm a list of topics that they might want to explore. My list consisted of my parent's divorce and my daughter's illness. I decided to write about my daughter's illness, but I had no idea where this project would go when it began. My instructor was Candace Reffe, a poet based in Provincetown, Massachusetts. "Where do I even start," I asked. Candace simply said, "Start at the beginning. Close your eyes and visualize the first image that comes to mind and go from there." So that is what I did. My first thought brought me back to when I started to fear something was wrong, and I wrote, "She slept more than the other five-month-old babies that I knew." I wrote on a yellow legal pad for the duration of the workshop, received helpful feedback and then when the workshop ended I kept going like Forest Gump who just kept running.

Every few months I would sit down and write the newest episode in the life of my family. I kept writing partly as an attempt to satisfy the desire to make sense of what was happening. I craved to know how other families dealt with serious illness and hunted for books and memoirs that had themes of survival and parenting a sick child. Without the internet that search was carried out in libraries and by reading book reviews. I was desperate for stories of how other families fared. How does this trauma impact a marriage? Will we laugh again? Can life go on? How do we raise this child with beautiful red hair and blue lips from cyanosis, and then, when her sister comes along, how do we deal with the inequities of one healthy child and another with a serious cardiac problem? We had a semblance of control over the medical care of our daughter but not the outcome. There was so much fear in the unknown.

Years went by and I continued to write but now my thoughts were typed and saved in a computer. I realized that, as Toni Morrison has said, I was writing the very book that I needed to read. It was written like a serialized Dickens novel. Each new entry was added contemporaneously, but I had no clue as to how or when this book would end . . . until I did.

This is not a funny story, yet, ironically, it is humor that got us through the worst of our experiences. We found humor in everyday mishaps and although my memory of the events in this book is crystal clear, I have very little memory of what made us laugh so hard and so often.

I hope this book will help others who are navigating the world of hospitals and doctor's offices. I hope this book will allow others to feel less alone. I hope this book will give hope to other families that you can endure one calamity after another and be knocked down but still maintain the strength to stand up and relish the joys of life.

I have learned that one catastrophe does not make you immune from the next. When I was a child, I remember thinking that since my parents were divorced, I would be protected from other disasters. But the nature of tragedy is indiscriminate. It gives no thought to who has suffered and does not dole it out evenly with a measuring cup. In this memoir I have not tried to address the question of why we suffer but rather how. It defines our character and shapes our lives.

Evil Phrase

I considered myself lucky. Dana slept more than the other five-month-old babies that I knew. I had time to read the paper and have a cup of coffee. My friends, also new moms, complained about a loss of personal time. I sympathized with them, but could not really understand what they were talking about.

My friends' babies were bottle-fed and getting chubbier by the day. My breast-fed baby was eating, but not gaining. She looked so lean. "They only take what they need," La Leche assured.

I had doubts.

My baby perspired at night and while she nursed. My sister told me that her three children had been heavy sweaters as babies and awoke with matted hair and clammy faces.

Somehow, I was not consoled.

Something was not right. Dana was not gaining weight. She was breathing heavily and napping constantly. Reading the newspaper during the day was lovely but I knew that having the time to get through the entire *New York Times* while she slept was not normal.

The pediatrician's initial reaction stung like a slap across my cheek.

Pneumonia.

It sounded so evil. Shame washed over me. I assumed, incorrectly, that pneumonia was a cold that had not been properly treated. I had been a neglectful mother. The thought pushed me into a hole. In hindsight, I marvel at the cruel irony. If only it could have been so simple.

The pediatrician called Babies' Hospital at Columbia Presbyterian and made an appointment for Dana to be seen as soon as possible. We lived in New Jersey; no one asked me if I was okay to drive. Dana was hysterically crying and by the time I got in the car, so was I. I screamed my way over the George Washington Bridge.

We were seen by Dr. Margaret Kenert, a pediatric cardiologist. Soon, an x-ray revealed that Dana had an abnormally enlarged heart; a warning sign that something was very wrong.

Enlarged heart. More evil words.

Dana was admitted to the hospital and an emergency catheterization was scheduled for the following day. This is a procedure in which a catheter is snaked into an artery to reveal cardiac abnormalities. A young fellow, a medical specialist, was tasked with informing us about all the calamities that could befall our baby during this procedure. He sat across an empty desk. On it was a useless ink blotter and dirty take-out cup from a nearby coffee shop. The cold fluorescent light above hissed and blinked. His tone of voice was matter-of-fact as if he were reciting a list of car problems to his mechanic. He took the consent form he had just reviewed with us and slid it across the desk for my husband, Steve, and me to sign. We expected to never see Dana again.

We were feeling physically ill. My heart was pounding and I could not warm up. Steve's complexion paled, and he felt nauseous. We walked to a balcony overlooking the Hudson River. The New York skyline to the south used to represent everything that the world had to offer. From our vantage point we could see the Empire State Building. It reminded me of when my grandmother took my sister and me to the very top. The whole world spread out below us. I could not see Radio City Music Hall from where I stood, but I imagined waiting in line, for what seemed like hours, to catch the Christmas Show and see the Rockettes kick; now those memories and the view of the skyline represented all that we would never be able to do with our baby. This realization made the anticipated loss I was feeling real. We waited in silence for an hour that felt like years.

Finally, we learned the procedure was successful — Dana had made it through! Unfortunately, no sooner could we celebrate than the results dealt us a harsh truth: Dana had a severe congenital heart defect known as Transposition of the Great Vessels, in which the position of the two major vessels that carry blood away from the heart is switched.

I prayed she would not need an operation.

Following "pneumonia" and "enlarged heart," the new evil phrase became "open-heart surgery." These words made me sick inside. Could I bear the thought of my baby's little breastbone being cut open, or the sight of a scar down the center of her silken skin? But soon those evil words transformed into a fervent — even desperate — prayer. *Please let there be an operation for her.* This evil phrase, which on a previous day landed like a punch, quickly and paradoxically caressed me the next. Open-heart surgery were the words I most wanted to hear as my husband and I sat in front of Dr. Kenert, awaiting her detailed diagnosis and prognosis of what options were available in 1977. A sickness was churning inside me and my breath became shallow. Even though the calendar told me it was mid May, I was shivering. Outside of Dr. Kenert'swindow, I could see a Weeping Willow tree. Birds were chirping. Doctors were walking in and out of the garden entrance to Babies' Hospital at Columbia Presbyterian, conversing and laughing as if the world was still right side up. Gently, the doctor presented us with the results of the catheterization. With the instinct of self-preservation, I felt myself retreating from the harsh blow of her words. Mechanically, I responded or nodded at appropriate intervals. I played the part of the calm and collected adult. Inside, a tornado was brewing. Dana was going to be hospitalized for one week to stabilize her. Instead of open-heart surgery, she would have a minor operation within the next few months that could only stave off her continued congestive heart failure – not fix it. We were unsure as to why corrective surgery was not mentioned, although it is possible that that information was offered but floated in the air, too painful to process. Looking back, we only asked questions for which we were ready to hear the answer. A drug called Digoxin was administered to maintain her heart rate. The cardiologist told us that the operation would buy us time. There was one thought that echoed repeatedly in a dark recess of my brain . . .

Time for what?

Common Denominator

Since Steve still had to go to work each day, we determined that I would be the one to sleep at the hospital with Dana each night. That first night, I kissed my husband goodbye at the elevator, and walked back to Dana's room in a haze.

She was sleeping peacefully, oblivious to the beeps and whirrs of the machinery attached to her. I couldn't bring myself to lie on the cot, caged in by my thoughts, so I began what was the first mile of several hundred that I would log shuffling around the pediatric floor of Babies' Hospital. On my third or fourth trip around the nurses' station, I noticed a playroom with a television droning on in the corner. I popped in to try to lose myself in some mindless television sitcom. On one couch in the corner, a father snored loudly. Across the room, on one end of a wrap-around couch, sat a giant yellow Big Bird. He leaned off to one side, but seemed secure enough to remain firmly on the couch until morning, when he would be rested and ready for the children who came into the room to play. On the other end of that same couch sat three women in a tight little circle, leaning in and talking quietly so as not to disturb the snoring father. They looked over at me and whispered, "Come and join us."

I listened to the stories of each mother's child's diagnosis. I was the novice in the group; the other women had already spent the previous few nights together. One woman was Irish Catholic and had grown up in Indianapolis. She was single and had no family in the New York area. Her child was born without digestive organs. Another woman was from a royal Indian family and had grown up in what was then still called Bombay. She wore a purple Bindi dot on her forehead and a purple sari. Her jet-black hair was piled on top of her head in what I referred to in my childhood as a chignon. Her son had a congenital heart defect and was awaiting surgery the following morning. The third mother was from Laurelton, NY. She had just moved from Harlem. After discussing her daughter's diagnosis of sickle cell anemia, she lamented about missing the vibrancy of city life. By the time anyone looked at a watch, it was 3:00 AM. Energized by the conversation yet knowing that we needed to be alert in the morning to deal with the assaults of the upcoming day, we said our goodnights.

For the next eight nights, we "playroom ladies" met and talked. We revealed to each other our deepest fears — fears that we could not repeat to another soul. We talked about how our families were coping and in what ways they were being supportive . . . or not. Each of our family members was in pain and yet we could not bear their pain as well as our own. Although my family was supportive, they could not truly understand how I was feeling or what I was experiencing. Dana's diagnosis had set my husband and me adrift into the unexplored Sea of Serious Illness, a place our extended families could not enter. But the "playroom ladies" were there with me. I began to think of our little group, in some very important ways, closer to me than my family. We talked about how we were raised and knew that our cultural differences would have separated us in the "real world." On the surface, we all had absolutely no similarities. Our common denominator was more powerful than any of our differences.

We were all adrift together, bound by our sorrows and our fears. We inhabited a parallel world. We lived side-by-side with other parents of healthy children, but we were denied the simple pleasure of wondering and dreaming of our children's futures. What had happened to us was life-altering, and we knew that we would always be more like each other than our own relatives and friends. We were four mothers, racking up miles around and around the nurses' station, wearing an invisible rut in the linoleum that only the other mothers could see. We wait in playrooms and hospital rooms, we sleep on roll-away cots and pull-down beds, and we pray that our children live through the next storm.

The Curse

Quickly, Steve and I fell into a monotonous routine. I lived at the hospital that first week with Dana. At night, after work, he would drive up the West Side Highway and visit with us until fatigue overtook him. Then he would drive home to Fort Lee, mercifully close to the hospital, to sleep, and then start the whole thing all over again the next morning.

Aside from the mommies that we bonded with in the playroom, we became close with a woman named Lorraine. She was in an adjacent room with her four-year-old son, DJ; he was awaiting a very risky cardiac surgery. She told us that DJ's odds for survival were less than 50%. While we were inundated with relatives coming to visit, she was always alone in DJ's room. She seemed to have no one, so we welcomed her to spend time with us. We brought her food from the cafeteria and watched DJ when she needed to use the bathroom.

One afternoon, Steve, Lorraine, and I were sitting in Dana's room chatting when Steve's parents arrived for a visit. The moment they walked through the door Lorraine's face drained of color. She stood up abruptly and left the room without introduction. We gave her grace and assumed she left because she did not want to intrude, though we both thought her reaction was very odd.

The afternoon played out predictably. My in-laws played with Dana and badgered us with questions we were not ready to ask ourselves. Their visits always ended the same way: they would ask us to go to a local restaurant for dinner, knowing full well that we would not want to leave Dana alone, and then look visibly upset when we told them as much. They could have offered to stay with her while we went to the cafeteria downstairs for a much-needed respite, but they never did.

After they left, Lorraine returned to Dana's room. "Who was that woman?" she asked, slightly unnerved. When we told her, she became even more distraught. "I'm so sorry," she said.

We had no idea why.

"That woman," Lorraine began, clearly emotional, "was my assigned case worker when I applied for welfare." She wiped her face with a tissue. "I had to quit my job when DJ was born because he was in and out of the hospital, and my boss said he could not keep me on the payroll if I could not be a reliable worker. DJ's father had gone AWOL months before DJ was even born, and my parents own and run a dairy farm in St. Elmo, Illinois. I could not rely on them for financial or emotional support, and they could not leave the farm to be with us. Your mother was the case worker who came to my home."

Lorraine went through an entire small packet of tissues as she told her story. "I was desperate for financial help," she whispered. "I feared being evicted, and if it weren't for the measly amount of unemployment that I received, I don't know how I would've put food on the table." Lorraine took a deep breath and looked at Steve. "That woman did everything she could to prevent me from getting assistance. She somehow got it into her head that there was a father hiding somewhere who was perfectly capable of supporting us and that I was trying to pull this huge scam on the government. She made me jump through hoops to get multiple letters from DJ's doctors to prove that he was as sick as I claimed he was. It added months of delay on my ability to collect the food stamps and support I so desperately needed. She is evil. Anyone with one eye could look at DJ, see his blue lips and pale skin, and know immediately that something was very wrong."

Lorraine paused, staring through the window and out onto the Hudson River below us. Then she looked back at us briefly, and lowered her eyes to the floor. "Luckily," she continued, "I was able to get the agency to send another case worker and, ultimately, received the aid that I needed. But I cursed her. I wished this on her." Lorraine looked at Steve without malice. "I wished that she would have a sick child so she would know the anguish and sadness in her own heart. I'm sorry, but I did." Lorraine kept apologizing to us profusely and repeatedly. Steve and I were shaken to the core.

We were not surprised by her story. We knew that my mother-in-law could behave in exactly the way Lorraine described. It was not because she was without mercy or compassion, but because she was a concrete, literal thinker and had a job to do. She was on the lookout for fraud even when there was none. She was not a trained social worker. The county hired and provided one month of cursory training for people to go into the homes of applicants armed with clipboards and too much power. She had her questions to ask — "Just the facts, ma'am." She wanted to know where DJ's father was. She had the privilege of a husband and healthy children. She could not conceive of the hardships that less fortunate people like Lorraine had to endure.

The coincidence and the intertwining of our stories made the curse feel almost real. We prayed that DJ's surgery would be successful. We couldn't bear a different outcome. The next morning, thankfully, DJ's cardiologist said the surgical correction was successful. DJ would be able to go on living a normal life without restrictions. Within the week, DJ, who was running up and down the linoleum corridor pink-faced, was discharged. By the end of that first week, we, too, left the hospital with Dana in tow.

We never saw Lorraine again.

Stability

The new word of the week was *stable*. My five-month-old daughter was stable. We came away from the hospital with a diagnosis and a multitude of new descriptive phrases. Now, when people would inquire what was wrong, I could say, "Yes, she has Transposition of the Great Vessels, and she is stable." It sounded good. It had a catchy ring to it. If it had such an important sounding name, it could be understood. It could be corrected. Couldn't it?

When I was a child, my parents separated and I could not wait for them to be divorced. "Divorced" was a word more people understood. The word "separated" left the door open for foolish people to ask, "Will they get back together?" "Divorced" was authoritative. It had finality. Everyone understood that that door was shut. So, too, was it shut with the "Transposition of the Great Vessels"; a definitive diagnosis kept people from asking the most frightening questions.

Because Dana remained stable, our lives resumed a normal routine in surprisingly little time. I lived the life of any other typical stay-at-home mom. I had other friends who, like me, were on maternity leave from teaching, and I made plans for us to do all the activities we had never had time for before. We went to playgroups and out to lunch. We went to the Museum of Natural History. The museum conveniently allowed strollers and had a private room for nursing mothers.

My college roommate, Annie, lived in the city. Together we would pile Dana and Annie's son, Josh, (Dana's soon-to-be lifelong friend), into the umbrella strollers and set out for the streets of New York City. We would stroll up Madison Avenue buying cookies and chocolates and would hang the shopping bags on the handles of the strollers. When each kid fell asleep, we would drive their strollers into the Carlyle Hotel and treat ourselves to a late afternoon glass of wine. We called them our "afternoon teas." We were always the only ones in their historic Bemelman's Bar; while the kids snoozed contentedly, we laughed and gossiped until the weight of the shopping bags started to tip over one or both strollers.

Aside from a visit to Dr. Kenert's every three months, Dana was stable enough for me to forget about Lorraine's curse, which had been lingering in the back of my mind since we came back from the hospital. I became comfortable enough to take her for her check-ups without Steve, my guide through the maze of hospital corridors. I joked with the nurses and doctors. I was relaxed and funny. From a doctor's point of view, I thought I was a real pleasure to have as a patient's mom. I thought, if they liked me, they would care for my daughter better. Though desperation lurked under the surface of my smile, I did not let them see it.

Occasionally, something would happen to pull me back into my reality. One day, I was waiting in the supermarket check-out line. Dana was chomping on a bagel and babbling happily in her stroller. An elderly woman in front of me peered down at Dana disapprovingly. The longer she stared, the more uncomfortable I became. Next, she locked eyes with me; I could see hers were full of daggers.

"This child is too pale!" She scolded. "She needs sunlight. Don't you ever take her to a playground?"

Her words felt like a kick to my stomach.

My mouth hung open and I began to cry. "She's not pale, she's sick!" I screamed. "You dare to speak about my child whom you don't even know? Shame on you."

What would cause a stranger to speak to me like that? Did she think she was being helpful? I thought of the old 1950s game show, "Kids Say the Darndest Things." The moderator, Art Linkletter, would interview children about various things; their answers were refreshingly candid and uninhibited. This stranger's comment was not only candid and uninhibited, it was rude and inappropriate. She knew nothing about my life, yet she spoke as if she knew my daughter and believed she had the right to offer her "diagnosis." In these moments, the feeling of being adrift and alienated on the Sea of Serious Illness washed through me.

Nightmare

Before I had Dana, I rarely suffered from insomnia. Sleep had always been a friendly haven into which I had been mercifully able to escape at the end of each day. But during those early months after Dana's diagnosis, I was plagued by a vivid, repeating nightmare.

Every night, a faceless entity chased me as I ran towards a soaring tower, which was precariously situated on a cliff. I found safety, for a time, within the tower's wooden frame. My lungs ached from gulping huge breaths of air. I was sure this evil entity had followed the sound of my pounding heart. Once inside the tower, I bolted the door against it and saw a wooden ladder that wound around in sharp curves. It ascended at a sheer vertical pitch toward the top platform. I knew if I made it to the landing, the entity would not be able to reach me. I didn't understand why it was following me; I had done nothing wrong. Who was this faceless beast?

Eventually, I would reach solid ground high up in the tower, but still I was not safe. There, I was accosted by The Women. Each one was identical to the next; each woman wore the same baby blue, pin-striped uniform, each one the same rimless glasses. They popped up through the floorboards like that classic arcade game,

Whack-a-Mole. But this was no game. Instead of a mallet, I had a revolver. I pivoted quickly, keeping my back to one of the four openings that led out to the balcony, and shot down every single menacing female.

Finally, the frantic assault of The Women ceased, and I could breathe for the first time. I backed onto the balcony, which wrapped around the entire tower. Its surface was made from loosely fitted beams of wood, through which I could see the jagged ground hundreds of feet below. I looked out over the rickety railing and saw a large body of water; it sparkled like thousands of diamonds reflecting the blinding sun. For a moment, I felt like Jimmy Stewart in the movie "Vertigo," but dizziness was not the sensation I experienced. Instead, with the faceless entity and The Women safely dispatched, I felt a momentary lightness — a lifting of a monumental burden — that was rejuvenating. Powerful, even. Each night in my dreams, I outran a faceless predator and single-handedly murdered countless hateful women. I knew the feeling of safety was ephemeral, but I felt euphoric. Each night in my dreams, I was a mass murderer. I fought off the evil forces just like I escaped the curse.

I also felt ashamed. Night after night, week after week, I awoke in a sweat. My days were plagued by the fear that when I did finally fall asleep, I would get no rest. I feared sleep, and yet I craved it. For the first five months of Dana's life, before the Sea of Serious Illness, before the Transposition of the Great Vessels, I was the mother of a beautiful red-headed, blue-eyed baby girl. I drank up each coo, gurgle, and giggle; it was our own little language. I dreamed the dreams of all mothers, and wondered who she would be, what things she would laugh at, where would life take her. No matter how normal our routine may have seemed, those dreams for Dana were dead, and I deeply mourned their loss. Instead of planning for college, I prayed that she would live.

One day, while Dana had been admitted to the hospital for tests, catheterizations, and blood work, I noticed the setting sun beaming through her hospital window. There were no shades to block the glare; only vertical blinds trapped within two panes of glass and a useless wand dangling from the top pane. From the seventh floor of Babies' Hospital we had a perfect view of the Hudson River. It was a view I used to love. I grew up on the other side of the river, a bit further south. I spent my childhood walking up the block from my house to the river whenever I needed peace or solitude. At this time of day, the sun caught the white caps on the river in a dazzling display of light. But the solace I once derived from this view had been replaced by a feeling of inexplicable dread.

The sun had begun its descent behind the high-rise buildings of Fort Lee, New Jersey. It was getting close to the time that Steve would walk into our daughter's hospital room after wending his way up the West Side Highway from work. It was at this time of day, as well, that Dr. Kenert would arrive for her evening rounds. I heard her heels clicking on the linoleum as she arrived with her retinue of medical students, interns, and residents in their uniforms. I had seen them huddled in the hall discussing the prognosis of their previous patient. I could tell the interns from the residents by their bright-eyed and bushy-tailed demeanor, their hair bundled tightly in buns, and their feet sunk into flat, sensible shoes. They leaned into the circle of medical personnel to soak up every word.

Dr. Kenert entered the room. She briefed her retinue and explained to us the results of whatever new tests had been performed that day. As the sun glinted off of her rimless glasses, images of the Women from my dream popped into my mind. Immediately, I knew who the faceless predator and the Women were. I understood what chased me in my dreams, what haunted my sleep. If only the answer was as simple as pulling out a revolver and shooting the messenger of unbearable news.

That night, I finally slept.

Buying Time

We followed the advice of Dana's doctors. Aside from the procedures and tests that were performed on her during her stays, which varied from overnight to a week, we made the experience as pleasant as possible. The hospital had a wonderful playroom where we spent countless hours, and each floor in Babies' Hospital had a kitchen where parents could get a cup of coffee for themselves or store food from home. I made sure to always have Nestle® Nesquick® on hand and Kraft Macaroni and Cheese, which I would make at home and bring to the hospital to be reheated for when Dana would refuse to eat the hospital food.

Each Wednesday, the parents of a former patient would arrive at the playroom and transform it into an English Garden. Their son had been a patient years before and this was their way of paying back for the care that he had received. They spent an hour wrapping realistic-looking, plastic garlands of ivy around the perimeter of the room and placed flowered tablecloths over the children's formica tables. With the help of a nurse, the mom stood precariously on a ladder while she thumb-tacked flowered fabric over the fluorescent lights. When they had completed this transformation, the English Garden was open for business. Along with the decorations, they provided homemade tea sandwiches (with the crusts removed, of course) and a green salad. Patients and their parents filed into the room; some patients were wheeled in a wheelchair and others walked slowly, pushing their IV poles. Classical music played softly in the background. It may not sound like much. It may sound like too much work for one hour of English Garden Tea Time. But the change was a respite from the sterile, cold light of the hospital. The air in the room was transformed, and for a brief time the children and parents could forget where they were.

It was lovely.

When not in the hospital, we adapted to our new life. But the mind is a complex and intricate blend of elements. It valiantly protects its organism from information it knows the host cannot handle. Steve had heard our daughter's prognosis two years before, it floated on the surface of his mind, pulling him down into a deep depression. I, on the other hand, had attached a large stone to the diagnosis of Transposition of the Great Vessels and watched it sink down into the quicksand of my subconscious. I was well aware of the gravity of Dana's diagnosis and its implication for her future, but the emotion that should have accompanied that knowledge was out of my grasp; it seemed separated by an invisible membrane. I wasn't sure if this inability to emote was a coping super power or if there was something lacking in my emotional make-up.

At Dana's two-year-old checkup, Dr. Kenert and I finally spoke openly about her developmental milestones. Dana played by my side with toys that were strewn around the office, while

Dr.Kenert, in a soothing voice, explained to me Dana's unspoken prognosis. "The pulmonary pressure caused by her heart defect is also affecting her lungs. There is no operation that can repair her heart. The previous surgery is buying her time. It is keeping her stable so that when she needs something, *hopefully*, there will be something. At this point, what we need to look forward to is a heart transplant."

My face was wet with tears. Did she know that this information was foreign to me? Did she allow me the last two years of blissful ignorance so I could heal from the initial blow of not having a healthy baby?

The year was 1979.

There had yet to be a heart transplant that resulted in longevity.

Cuckoo's Nest

Preparing Dana for the hospital visits was relatively simple when she was so young. We bought every picture book we could find to help explain things to Dana: *My Visit to the Hospital, Curious George Goes to the Hospital,* and *Hospital Story.* We bought Baby Heartbeat, the doll whose battery-operated stethoscope allowed one to hear a mechanical *lub-dub.* Baby Heartbeat would always get her injections and EKG before Dana. It did not stop Dana's screaming, but it cajoled us into thinking that we were in some small way easing her pain. I hope we were right.

On the long hospital stays, we never left her side — night or day. In times of crisis, any small act of thoughtfulness or consideration is magnified. There are doctors, nurses, and technicians who will never know how much I cherished their kindness. But one particular evening, after enduring an emotional tornado of yet another catheterization, I made what I thought was a simple request to the nurse on night duty. It was 9:00 PM. and I was exhausted. At that time, each room in Babies' Hospital was equipped with a bed for a parent that folded down from the wall like a Murphy bed. One needed a key to release the latch. The keeper of the key on that night came straight out of a horror movie, like the cold-hearted nurse in the movie, "One Flew Over the Cuckoo's Nest."

"May I please have the key to pull down the bed?" I asked her. Her response was so slow in coming that I had to repeat my request three times.

"NO," she snapped. "Can't you see I'm busy?"

She was not busy, but I felt totally intimidated. I shuffled back to the room, the solace of sleep delayed. By 10:15, my fatigue had transformed into anger. So out I went for the fourth and final time.

"Give me the key, you despicable bitch. Give me the God-damned key."

Big dogs back down if you bark back loudly enough. But, as I lay in bed that night, I still churned with anger and incredulity. Why would a nurse whose literal job it was to be nurturing, be so cold? Didn't she understand how vulnerable I was? Did she have any idea how her cruelty ripped through me? I made up my mind that night, as I listened to the whirring and beeping of the machines that were attached to my baby: I would never be intimidated again.

Dana was in and out of various hospitals seven times during the first four years of her life. In that time, we sought out second, third, and fourth doctor's opinions, from New York all the way to California. We always received the same grim news — the same bottom line: "95% of all congenital heart defects are operable. Unfortunately, your daughter is in the other 5%."

But Dr. Kenert had said one thing that I remembered very clearly. "When Dana needs something," she told me, "there will be something."

Beware of Superstars

Steve's four years of dental school and three years of oral surgical residency equipped him with the knowledge to understand and navigate his way around all the medical jargon. He researched all the possible treatments for Dana's diagnosis. He kept coming upon studies that had been done at Stanford Medical Center in California. A doctor named Melvin Johnson was doing experimental surgery on children with Transposition of the Great Vessels; we made an appointment to fly to Palo Alto to see him.

Before we left, we discussed our plan with Dr. Kenert. "Dr. Johnson is very accomplished. He's the chief of Pediatric Cardiac Surgery at Stanford and is considered prominent in this field. But, beware of superstars." We did not know what she meant then, but those words would come back to haunt us.

We scheduled our trip to Stanford to coincide with the bar mitzvah of my cousin Arlene's son, Andy. We planned to go first to Stanford and then fly down to San Diego, where the bar mitzvah would take place a week later. Another cousin of mine, Jay, and his wife, Nancy Lee, had both attended Stanford Medical School. They accompanied us to Stanford to help us navigate the system and decipher the Great Dr. Johnson's opinion.

Dana was admitted to Stanford for another cardiac catheterization, and we were scheduled to meet with the doctor the following day to receive the results and hear his recommendation. The catheterization revealed the same information as the procedure at Babies' Hospital: the obstacle to a successful surgery was Dana's high pulmonary pressure. However, Dr. Johnson offered to "go in" and see what the heart really looked like with the naked eye; it was a risky surgery but perhaps it would reveal something he could do. He did not promise much, but he warned us if we did nothing, Dana would die within the year. He shook our hands and told us to go home and think about our decision.

We were horrified by the casualness with which he delivered this devastating news. We didn't want to let this man anywhere near our daughter. Shortly after the meeting, Jay and Nancy Lee confirmed our gut instincts. They said he offered nothing but euthanasia. As we left, Dr. Kenert's words rang in our ears: Beware of superstars.

From Stanford, we flew to San Diego with Jay and Nancy Lee for the festivities. I, fortunately, was able to compartmentalize my feelings and kept them outside that invisible membrane that allowed me to function as if everything was normal. I laughed and danced with our relatives and made sure that Dana, who was precociously intuitive, enjoyed herself. Her older cousins swung her around and cheered her on as she ran headfirst under the Limbo Stick, "The Limbo Song" by Frankie Anderson ringing out in the background. The bar mitzvah celebration was a reminder to balance what would surely be a lifetime of fear and sorrow with as much fun and frivolity as possible.

Too Much Emotion

Steve and I were firm believers in telling Dana the truth. We never lied, but we never exactly spelled out the bottom line for her either. As a teacher, I knew that children asked questions according to their level of understanding. We had years to go before Dana would mature enough to start asking the hard questions. However, we were also blessed with a precocious child. At the time, Steve was an attending oral surgeon at New York Hospital. He consulted a famous child psychiatrist on staff there regarding how to deal with Dana's questions and hospitalizations. He told Steve that the greatest fear for young, hospitalized children is abandonment. His advice was to keep our answers simple and honest, and to always be physically there for her, no matter what.

At age three, she wanted to know why she got breathless so quickly. A favorite activity of the nursery school set was to run up three front stairs of the building and jump off the statue of a lion into the grass below. She was very well aware that all of her nursery school friends could accomplish this feat with ease. Each child would roll in the grass, pick themselves up and start the process all over again. But after running up the three little stairs, Dana had to stop and rest before she could jump from the statue, and she wanted to know why. I explained that she was born with a heart that had been improperly formed. I used an analogy of hot water coming out of the cold-water faucet to explain her transposed vessels. I explained that her heart couldn't pick up enough oxygen to carry around her body, which was why she had blue lips and blue nails. All of this was delivered with a matter-of-fact tone. I thought too much emotion would scare her, so instead I showed no emotion. If I explained these analogies matter-of-factly, then maybe that would be how she would accept them. I was mistaken.

In first grade, she refused to learn how to spell the word heart. I quizzed her and taught her the trick of thinking about the word as the two words she could already spell "he" and "art." When the test rolled around, she spelled the word wrong anyway. This internal rebellion continued even into high school, when she refused to learn the required information on the heart for her biology test.

I soothed her when she cried, but I never let down my guard. I kept telling myself that too much emotion would scare her. I had replaced the phrase attached to the rock buried in my subconscious with a new phrase: Do not cry. Do not ever cry. But who was I kidding? Too much emotion scared me. I was afraid that if I cried, I would not stop. Ever. It wasn't until years later that I realized what message I had been sending my beloved daughter.

As she grew older, she got closer and closer to her target question: What is going to happen to me? Like Mohammad Ali, poking at an inferior boxer, Dana danced around the question that must have been on her mind. Dana knew exactly when the K.O. punch would come. The only reason she avoided it was to protect me.

At age seven, we told Dana that she would require more surgery someday.

"Why, Mommy?" she asked. "When?"

In soothing tones, I replied with a brief perfunctory explanation. "Not until you need it."

It was all I could say. I thought that if I continued to evade Dana's questions, I could still deny my reality. Instead, my reluctance to face the truth instilled in her a fierce fear of the future. If there was information that was taboo, it must be too dreadful to hear. How could I expect her to accept who she was and what she would need to face in her life without giving her the facts? I began by learning how to be honest with myself first. I had to conquer my fears, otherwise how could I help her to conquer hers?

Through the hard times, I kept one event in my mind when I needed a heaping dose of optimism. Steve and I belonged to a support group called Young Hearts — for parents of children with congenital heart defects, sponsored by the Red Cross. One of the organizers of the support group was a mother whose daughter, Alison, had undergone several open-heart surgeries. One night, her child came to the meeting to share her perspective as a patient with the group. I gaped in amazement at the fifteen-year-old high school student standing before me. She told us all about her surgeries and times when her parents feared for her survival.

She talked about some of the limitations in her life as a result of her cardiac issue. I remember thinking, you mean you can live with this? You can get to be a teenager?

It was the first time I felt a glimmer of hope.

Luxury Problems

Although Dana remained physically small for her age, she was extremely mature and verbally advanced. Evelyn, her pre-kindergarten teacher, thought Dana was gifted. Because of her small size, I was able to keep her in the umbrella stroller far longer than if she had grown typically. When people heard her speak with such sophisticated language, they looked for the ventriloquist voicing her words.

Life went on. I became pregnant again. Steve and I were both fearful that this new baby would suffer the same fate as Dana. At an appointment with Dr. Kenert, I asked if she could listen to my unborn baby's heartbeat. She wouldn't do it. She said that there was no medical reason to think that a congenital heart defect would happen to our second child.

When Dana was four and a half years old, I gave birth to Jacqueline. While She was easy going and adorable, and giggled easily and often, the glaring difference between Dana and Jacqueline was the predictability with which Jackie reached each developmental stage. Jacqueline sat up, rolled over, gained appropriate weight, and walked at exactly the stage when the child development books said she would.

Dana became jealous of Jackie even before we brought her home from the hospital. When I went into labor, at 6:00 AM. on June 19th, 1981, and left for the hospital, Dana sat at the front door and wailed for hours. My mother brought her to Toys R Us and let her pick out whatever toys she wanted. Part of her fear, I believe, was that she knew I was going to a hospital; a place that held only frightening thoughts and this new baby was the reason. One night, I was diapering Jackie and kissing her belly to make her laugh. Out of the corner of my eye I saw Dana, standing in the doorway glaring, as if she had found me doing something unspeakable. But sibling rivalry, as fierce as it can be, was still a luxury problem.

I paid it little mind.

Damaged Goods

When Dana entered public school in first grade, we added a new list of evil words and phrases to our vocabulary: gym, recess, kickball, relay races, roller skating parties, to name a few. Public schools are not equipped to handle children like Dana. She always felt different and on the outside looking in.

Dana had very little stamina. For her, running from first to second base was the equivalent of running a mile. On the first day of school, Dana's first-grade class was scheduled for gym. I had taken great pains to pre-arrange an alternative for Dana. I told the principal in June that I wanted Dana scheduled for something else during gym, such as art or music. The principal was six months away from retirement and did not seem to care enough to remember. The first-grade teacher meant well, but she had no alternate plan. Dana watched as the other kids skipped off to gym, while she was escorted to the place where the kids are sent when they misbehave: the Principal's Office.

It stung Dana like a slap to her cheek. Her first slap. This was quickly and inevitably followed by many more:

"I'll race you to the water fountain." *Slap.*

"Let's play jump rope." *Slap.*

This was the very business of childhood — running, jumping, skipping, hopping.

By the end of the first month of school, Dana was learning that she was different. When teams were chosen during lunch or recess, she was either picked last or told blatantly that she was not wanted. My blue-eyed, red headed girl who loved to read, play Barbies with her sister, and write stories was seen as an obstacle on any team.

All throughout elementary school, Dana had had difficulty relating to the girls in her class, and they could not relate to her. What did they understand about being frequently hospitalized? Did they comprehend that for her to stroll around town after school and walk to friends' houses would require a much slower walking pace, and frequent stops for her to rest and catch her breath? Because of her physical limitations, the girls in Dana's class had interests that were completely different from hers. They wanted to go and do and run and skip. She wanted to do any activity that was sedentary.

It was not long before she expected people to react to her negatively. Her self-image was suffering, and we feared that she was beginning to think of herself as damaged goods. As a child of divorce, I remember having a recurring fantasy that if I were better behaved or smarter, or if I had been a boy instead, my father would not have left us. I made an erroneous leap of reason, so typical of children of divorce, that I had somehow caused their divorce.

One night before bed, I told Dana about how I had felt as a child. I asked her if she ever felt that way, that she had somehow caused her own heart problem. Though Dana complained and whined plenty, she, like her mother, rarely cried. That night, she burst into uncontrollable sobs. "Yes," she wailed, "Yes."

My heart ached. I hugged her tightly hoping the love she received at home would compensate for her limitations.

We moved from Fort Lee to nearby Tenafly, New Jersey, when Dana was nine-and-a-half and Jackie was four. Each town has its share of mean girls, and Tenafly was no different. Within a week of the change, the feeling of alienation that Dana had previously felt in her old town was reinforced in her new town. The children in her class had a vague idea that something was amiss when gym time rolled around. Dana mumbled something about a heart condition as her class filed out of the classroom. She then joined the other third grade class in Art — a substitution I made sure would happen this time. At lunch, during that first week in her new school, my daughter — the new kid — went to sit with her classmates, and one of them sneered and said, "You can't sit here. You have a heart problem."

Slap.

How could I soothe her aching heart? How could we give her the support she needed? Throughout the early days of the crises, although my family and friends could not understand what I was going through, they wrapped me in love and support. My friends set up a "hotline" for news about Dana's condition after each hospitalization. My mother showed up at the hospital one day and demanded the keys to my apartment so she could do the laundry. The first time that Dana was hospitalized, my sister and brother-in-law, who lived forty-five minutes outside of Manhattan and had only just returned at 9:30 PM that night from a trip abroad, walked into Dana's hospital room. It was 10:15 PM. This was support.

But who did Dana have? These new children who feared and rejected her?

"Can she die?" *Slap.*

"Is it catchy?" *Slap.*

"Can I die?" *Slap.*

Many years later, on a checkout line in CVS®, I encountered the sneering girl who had prevented Dana from sitting with her class in the cafeteria and continued to torment her through middle school. She was married with three screaming children hanging on her. She waved from her spot in the line adjacent to mine. I wanted to say, "I hope other kids will be kinder to your children than you were to mine." But I did not. I just turned around and paid for my items and left the store.

Two Steps Forward

All along this road through denial and toward acceptance, there was Jackie — listening, observing, learning. Jackie was the quintessence of each age she had been. To a mother who angrily ripped apart the child development handbook, *The First Year of Life*, in a teary frustration, it seemed that Jackie was the child about whom this book was written. She was everything that Dana was not; athletic, popular, easy going, and artistically talented. When it was time for Jackie's kindergarten conference, I expected to hear accolades — and there were some.

But there was also something else.

"Jackie seems withdrawn," her teacher, Mrs. Saydah, said compassionately. "I pulled her onto my lap the other day and asked her if anything was wrong. She told me she was worried about her sister, who has a heart problem."

Jackie was our wise watcher, the one who filled our voids with cheer and laughter, what an enormous burden for a little girl to bear. Dana did not respond well to her sister, this golden child. In my friend Debbie's backyard, I watched as Dana tried with all her strength to pull herself up on the rings of the swing set. She tried and failed six times before giving up. Jackie, seizing the chance to play on something new, grabbed onto the rings, pulled herself up, and flipped over.

Although sibling rivalry is normal, it was a misnomer for my children. There was no rivalry. Rivalry is the word for competition between two who are nearly equal. With these sisters, there was no equality. Jacqueline could; Dana could not. Jackie adored Dana, but Dana resented her sister with an intensity that was palpable. This could lead to nothing but trouble.

I worried about what Dana's heart defect would do to her, physically.

I worried about the psychological effect of the unrelenting rejection on her fragile self-esteem.

I worried about the emotional effect that the constant focus and attention on Dana would have on Jackie.

I could cope with many things, but I was reaching my limit. I didn't think I could handle my daughters' complex and burdened relationship on my own. Steve and I decided it was time for professional intervention. We were not qualified to be therapists for our own children. After all, we were part of the problem.

Our pediatrician recommended a family therapist. Ruth, our therapist, brought us through the first leg of many tumultuous years. It was there, in the safety of that office, that Dana was finally allowed to give a voice to her deepest fears. Inside Ruth's office, sitting on the floor, hiding behind a chair, Dana finally let go.

"I'm afraid that if I laugh with my friends, I'll stop breathing."

"I'm afraid to let people get close."

"What if I die?"

Over a three-year period, some of Dana's demons were released. She finally began to relax. She stopped blaming her sister. Jackie, too, was able to vent her frustrations and for the first time revealed that she thought Dana received more attention. I started taking Jackie out for ice cream every Monday after school and that helped to make her feel special. We each took two steps forward and, occasionally, one back; not always using the best coping skills. But we learned how to communicate more openly with each other most of the time. We could not know the future, but we proceeded with more optimism.

The Fontan

Most families celebrate their children's birthdays. They may throw elaborate birthday parties. They may take a video of every gift that is unwrapped, every candle that is blown out. But they do not celebrate with the intensity and the underlying urgency and gratitude that we did. Each birthday was a gift, attended by our large extended families and Dana's classmates. Some parties were held in restaurants, but as Dana got older there were chocolate-making parties and gala events at the local roller rink. All the adults in attendance knew that these birthdays might be tragically finite. This was not something that was spoken. An outsider would see an ordinary birthday party with the requisite cakes and cookies and hilarity. But all who knew would see the underlying anxiety to celebrate a milestone that is not taken for granted.

In 1989, Dana was twelve years old. Her health had remained stable while she was taking Digoxin and several other cardiac medicines, but the blue lips and nails — called cyanosis, which were caused by less oxygen being pumped to her body from her heart — were becoming more pronounced. Because there had been so little in the change of her condition over the years, she had not had a catheterization or echocardiogram during her bi-annual doctor's visits in seven years. Dr. Kenert ordered an EKG for the up-coming visit. High pulmonary pressure was the underlying reason that she was not a candidate for surgery. However, in the previous seven years, EKG technology had advanced to a point where pulmonary pressure could now be calculated without the invasiveness of a catheterization.

On a warm spring day, during Dana's check-up, I sat with her in a darkened room during the EKG. A window was open at one end of the room from which I could hear birds chirping. I watched the television monitor that displayed the inner workings of my daughter's heart. To my untrained eyes, the image of it looked like two little girls holding hands and jumping rope. Dr. Kenert poked her head into the examining room and looked over the shoulder of the EKG technician. She casually glanced at the screen. But suddenly, there was a commotion. More doctors were called into the room. People seemed excited by what they saw, but I had no idea why. No one spoke to me or to Dana. We became invisible, and I was terrified. In Dana's twelve years of life, the only good news we had been given was in the form of that one word: stable. Finally, Dr. Kenert told us that Dana's pulmonary pressure was lower and no one knew why. Was this good news or bad? Was this what we had been buying time for? At last, we were told that Dana was now a candidate for corrective surgery. After the appointment, we flew to the nearest payphone and called Steve in his office. I screamed the news into the phone and had to repeat myself three times before he understood what I was saying.

We were elated.

We went about the task of finding a surgeon who would perform the very complicated procedure, known as the Fontan. Steve became a one-man research team, a Consumer Reports for cardiac surgeons. We met with Dr. Bowman, at Columbia Presbyterian, who had performed a procedure on Dana years before. We liked him. We trusted him. He painted a rosy picture; he thought she would do very well. Steve asked him how many of these surgeries he performed per year, and he said his average was twenty. Steve asked him who he would trust with his own daughter's life. He suggested Dr. Dennison at the Mayo Clinic in Rochester, Minnesota. All of the other resources that Steve consulted had also recommended Dr. Dennison. It was a match.

Steve, Dana, and I flew out to Minnesota to interview the surgeon. We flew out early in the morning and would fly home that night. I was so preoccupied that I neglected to call my school to let them know that I would be absent.

My mother took care of Jackie for the day, and we skipped off to the airport. Steve and I felt like Dorothy and the Tin Man skipping through the flowers on their way to Oz after they awoke from the Wicked Witch's spell. But Dana was ambivalent. She was terrified of the prospect of open-heart surgery, yet hopeful that her heart abnormality could be corrected.

The previous week, Dana had been walking her friend's golden retriever. She had wrapped his leash around her wrist. When her friend's mother came out of the house, the dog took off down the street with Dana still attached to the leash at the wrist. She was fortunate to not break any bones, but she needed stitches in her knee, which made it painful to walk. Her face and legs were black and blue. She must have looked like a battered child when we entered Dr. Dennison's office, pushing Dana in a wheelchair.

Compared to the kind bedside manner of Dr. Bowman, Dr. Dennison was cold and aloof. The picture he painted was far from rosy. He enumerated all the problems that could arise during the surgery. The complication that turned my blood cold was that she could have a stroke during the surgery. Slap. His description of the recuperation — if she survived the surgery — was similarly bleak. I had visions of Dana in that wheelchair long after the stitches in her knee were removed; living the life of an invalid. *Slap. Slap.*

He anticipated problems; but then he told us what could be done for each anticipated complication. As the interview ended, Steve asked him how many Fontan procedures he performed per year. He said his average was two hundred. As we left his office, Steve and I knew that we would entrust him with Dana's life.

After our meeting with Dr. Dennison, we went out for lunch. Steve ordered a chocolate shake. In an attempt to spoon the big lump of chocolate ice cream at the bottom of the glass into his waiting mouth, he tipped the glass at a steep angle. The glob of ice cream oozed slowly out and then plopped down onto his face. The three of us doubled over in laughter. It was exactly what we needed.

The surgery was scheduled for the middle of August. We spent the two months that led up the surgery in a trance. It was the end of the school year. I dutifully graded papers, administered final exams, and prepared the report cards for the last day of school. But I had a perpetual stomach ache and difficulty catching my breath. Steve's normally pale skin was ashen from fear, but he went to the office each day and performed oral surgical procedures on his patients. Jackie, who was finishing third grade, knew that her sister would be having a "procedure," but she was oblivious to the seriousness of the situation. We worried that telling her about Dana's surgery would be too much for Jackie to comprehend, too much for her to deal with at such a young age.

With Dana, we thought it would be best to present an open and positive front. We talked optimistically about the upcoming surgery — as if it were going to be a big adventure. She was, after all, twelve; old enough to know. She had sat through the same interview with Dr. Dennison and heard the same prognosis as we had, but somehow, she was still able to be upbeat and laugh. To this day, I have no idea how Dana coped.

One warm morning in late June, after school had let out, I was in my yard sipping coffee when I noticed something shiny poking up through the dirt. I dug it out with the tip of my sneaker and held it up. It was an authentic horseshoe, worn by a horse, not a horseshoe from a game. It seemed to me like a good omen. I brushed off the caked-on dirt and brought it into the house to clean. When we packed for our trip to the Mayo Clinic, the horseshoe was the first item that went into my suitcase.

Mayo Clinic

The Mayo Clinic is in Rochester, Minnesota. We flew first to Minneapolis and then boarded a prop jet to Rochester. Flying low over the farmlands of rural Minnesota, I pressed my nose to the window and took in the beauty of the lush fields below. I tracked the shadows of the clouds floating across the farmlands. Were they storm clouds or would they reveal silver linings? I stared out at the horizon and saw nothing but acres of green, peppered with the occasional farmhouse. These farmlands — the middle of nowhere — became our medical mecca, and we poured all our hope into this place.

Dana was admitted to St. Mary's Hospital, one of the two hospitals that comprised the Mayo Clinic, and Steve, Jackie, and I settled ourselves into the Bell Tower Hotel for what we anticipated would be three or four weeks. It was across the street from the hospital situated on a block lined with small hotels just like ours. They were all designed for the out-of-towners who flocked to Rochester from all parts of the world, as if it were Lourdes, hoping for a medical miracle. Steve and I needed moral support and help with Jackie, so we had worked out a schedule whereby each family member was assigned a specific date. This way, when one group left, another came to take its place. My sister, Helen, her husband, Mark, and Steve's sister, Randy, flew in that first night and stayed in rooms right down the hall from us.

Dana's surgery had been scheduled for 9:00 AM. that next morning, but it got postponed three times. Instead of early morning, we all had to wait an interminably long morning and even longer afternoon. Dana was not permitted to eat before the surgery; she was starving and petrified. We tried to distract her with board games and television. The wait was agonizing.

One of the fears that Dana had was that she wouldn't know if she had survived when she awoke from the anesthesia. It seemed irrational to us, but she worried that with the dreamy state of consciousness from the anesthesia drugs and not being able to speak with a ventilator tube inserted in her throat, how would she know if she was alive? Dana loved all things chocolate, and Nestles Crunch in particular. We made a deal before the surgery that we would ask the nurse in the Recovery Room to tape a Crunch Bar to the IV pole so that would be the first thing she would see when she awoke. It was a symbol of survival.

When it was finally time for the nurses to wheel Dana away, Jackie climbed onto the gurney and sprawled on top of her, hugging her goodbye. That sight, hearing the word goodbye, broke the levees that were keeping our tears from flooding the hallway. The adults hugged one another and sobbed as we said our goodbyes to Dana. I saw the horrified look in Jackie's eyes; in an instant, she saw what we had not told her. I was witnessing her realize that this was no ordinary "procedure." Seeing the bewildered and terrified look on her face, I was riddled with doubt and guilt. She was alone in her fear; she wasn't privy to the information that we adults had. We had time to prepare, Jackie was left in limbo.

Jackie spent a good portion of her waking hours in the bathroom. The drama unfolding around her was the beginning of what would develop into a serious gastrointestinal issues. Like a weather barometer, Jackie's innards correctly reported her fears for her sister.

Throughout the never-ending hours of waiting for news of Dana's progress, Jackie drew happy smiley faces and posters for her sister.

"Way to Go!"

"Get Well Soon!"

"We Love You."

I disappeared into the world of words and worked my way through one crossword puzzle after another. Steve slept. That morning, Steve's sister, Randy, told us that she had mistakenly sprayed her hair with Right Guard deodorant. We thought it was hilarious. The fact that her hair actually looked good added to the comic relief of the moment.

I had good feelings about the outcome of the surgery. Deep down, I harbored the magical thought that the energy from so many friends, relatives, and acquaintances praying and sending healing vibes to Minnesota would keep Dana with us and insure a positive outcome. Occasionally, nurse-messengers — angels of mercy — would find us and report on the progress of the surgery.

"They've made the incision."

"She's on the heart-lung machine."

"They're closing up."

And then, at last: "They're moving her to the recovery room. You may see her now."

We flew into her room. We expected to see Dana lying in a bed, still asleep. We expected to see tubes. We expected surgical scars and bandages. But no amount of expectations could have prepared us for what lay before us. Dana's face and body were bloated to twice their normal size. Although she was unconscious, her eyes were bulging open, not blinking. She had so many tubes coming from every orifice. Jackie ran out of the room. I followed her, and as I did, the miracle registered that, for the first time in her life, Dana's coloring was pink!

Making Friends

We could not have prepared Jackie for how frightening Dana looked after the surgery because we were just as shocked as she was. I tried to console her by emphasizing the importance of Dana's pink lips and nails. "But she looks like Frankenstein," Jackie cried. I was at a loss as to how to explain that. Luckily, by the next morning, the swelling in Dana's face and body had improved, and she was conscious. She was still intubated, breathing through a ventilator, so she could not speak. But we could comfort her with our presence and she could communicate by writing in a notebook.

While Dana was in the competent healing hands of her surgeon, cardiologist, and ICU nurses, I had time to focus on Jackie. I spoke with a social worker who suggested we take Jackie to the Child Life Program at the hospital to see one of the social workers who specialized in supporting the patients' siblings. The following morning we brought Jackie to Catherine MacKenzie's office. Jackie walked in slowly with her head down. We sat outside the door. An hour later, Jackie came skipping out. It was clear that Jackie was able to unburden herself in the safety of Catherine's office.

In a separate session, Catherine told Steve and me to pay

attention to Jackie's needs. She told us that, although Jackie was only eight years old, complicated medical information could be simplified for her to understand; that way, she would not feel so alone and in the dark.

Spending hour after hour in a hospital waiting room provides ample opportunity for parents to commiserate with other parents, exchange tales of woe, and offer some solace. Luckily for Jackie, during the second week of our stay, the hospital provided her with something even better: a friend. Sarah was eight years old, and her three-year-old sister was also having surgery at the Mayo Clinic. Sarah and Jackie spent each day together with their Barbie dolls and many of the stuffed animals that poured in for Dana from members of our synagogue who had heard our story and prayed for her every Sabbath.

Each parent took turns bringing the girls out to get some fresh air and run around Mayo's beautiful grounds. Every day, Jackie and Sarah begged coins and threw them into the fountains with their wishes for their sisters. Jackie was, for the first time since Dana's surgery, spending less time in the bathroom. She was laughing and doing cartwheels down the long corridors. Dana's recuperation was progressing, and Jackie was relaxed and having fun with Sarah. Seeing Jackie's burden lifted buoyed my spirits and I happily watched Jackie entertain us with her jokes, imaginative play, and gymnastics routines that she'd learned from her classes back home.

Since Dana was doing relatively well, I chose an afternoon to devote completely to Jackie. Minnesota is known for its lakes, and Rochester boasted one of its own. Jackie and I rented a canoe and spent a few hours taking turns paddling around the beautiful lake, surrounded by a forest of pine trees. Jackie fed the geese that floated up to our boat, and we nibbled on peanut butter and jelly sandwiches while bobbing gently on the water. We let our canoe float with the gentle current.

When we were ready to return to the shore, the clouds blackened and a brisk wind whipped up. The wind was blowing in the opposite direction from the shore, and I found that the more I paddled, the further away we were. Luckily, before I could panic, a young man and his girlfriend paddled near us. He tethered his canoe to ours and towed us in. If he hadn't floated by, there's no telling what could have happened! Aside from that excitement, it was a perfect, lovely afternoon spent in the healing arms of nature.

Recuperation was not going well for Sarah's sister, Samantha, so we kept Sarah with us frequently and brought her to dinner with us each night. One night after dinner, we brought Jackie and Sarah back to our hotel room to play. Almost as soon as we arrived, we received a call to bring Sarah back right away. At the hospital, two social workers were waiting for us. One whisked Sarah away; the other told us that Sarah's parents had made the heart crushing decision to pull Samantha from the life support that had been keeping her alive for the past twenty-four hours.

Later that night, the family brought Sarah into Dana's room to say goodbye. Jackie was inconsolable. "How can you live without a sister?" She asked.

Jackie kept in touch with Sarah long after we returned from Mayo. The girls wrote letters to one another and sent each other photographs and drawings. Jackie often dreamed of Sarah and talked about her constantly. Jackie, like all of us, needed support. After all, who had Jackie leaned on for all this time other than us? Sarah, a peer, was Jackie's lifeboat on the stormy Sea of Serious Illness, and we were grateful for that.

Four or five months after we returned home from the Mayo Clinic, Steve found a weekend dental course to take in Kentucky, where Sarah and her family lived. The course was within an hour's drive from their home. He flew there with Jackie, and arranged to have Sarah's parents, Regina and Steve, pick her up and take her to their house for the weekend. While there, Jackie saw that even though Samantha wasn't there physically, she was in the air all around. Pictures of her adorned the refrigerator. The family shared funny stories, and Jackie watched Sarah laugh.

As we had hoped, that trip taught Jackie that even after losing a sister, life could go on. Twenty-five years later, we all came together and danced at Sarah's wedding.

Rough Recovery

After a few weeks of steady progress, Dana's recuperation from the Fontan procedure had slowed and became painful. Dr. Dennison had warned us of the inability of the heart to pump efficiently enough to clear fluid buildup from the lungs. This complication kept Dana hospitalized for two weeks more than what we had expected. We had already been in the hospital for six weeks. Steve's parents and mine had come and gone. Steve's brother, Uncle Michael, and Aunt Susann, had also come and gone. Now we were left wondering if this surgery had provided Dana with the correction she needed to live a normal life.

As promised, for each complication, Dr. Dennison had provided a remedy. This fluid buildup in the lungs was no different. Dana had thick rubber tubes protruding from each lung **through** holes in her chest. Attached to each rubber tube was a rectangular plastic box. These boxes collected the fluid that seeped from her lungs. The tubes, which went directly into each lung, needed to be kept airtight. To accomplish this, thick white tape was used to secure the tubes to the chest and keep air from entering. When she walked, Steve and I each carried a box so that she was relatively unencumbered.

Every afternoon, the nurse would enter Dana's room with her

cart. One wheel wobbled, so when the nurse steered it down the hall I could hear a distinct wocketa-wocketa as it rolled across the linoleum. That sound meant it was time to change the tape around the tubes in Dana's chest. Like Pavlov's dogs, Dana and I became conditioned; the moment we heard wocketa-wocketa, wocketa wocketa, my stomach wrenched, and Dana began to panic. The adhesive needed to be airtight, so when it was removed, it peeled off a thin layer of her delicate skin. New tape was secured and the next day, that tape was removed along with yet another layer of her skin. Rinse and repeat, day after day. It was torture.

Finally, after a week that seemed like months, a procedure was scheduled to stem the tide of fluid oozing into Dana's left lung, which was considered more serious than her right lung. The doctors allowed me into the procedure room with Dana, though I did not know why. With no anesthesia administered to Dana beforehand, a caustic substance was funneled into my daughter's weeping lung. The nurses rolled her around so the acidic fluid could flow into all areas of the lung and seal the lining. My daughter did not cry. I could have dealt with crying. Like a wild horse fleeing a burning barn, Dana's eyes were horror struck and her nostrils flared. I could barely catch my breath; it felt like the blood drained from my body. Even with all that we had been through, I had never felt more vulnerable and impotent than I did in that moment. I could not protect her. I could not calm her. I could simply stand there — arms limp at my sides, mouth agape.

Within a day, the drainage of the left lung subsided. Doctors were able to remove the rubber tube from one lung. One week later, the tube from the right lung was removed as well. Finally, after eight weeks, we were cleared to go home.

Rite of Passage

Dana was about to enter the seventh grade, an academically and emotionally difficult year for most twelve-year old kids, even under the best of circumstances. Having taught seventh grade for over twenty years, I knew better than most that social issues could bedevil even the most confident teenager.

Once home, the recuperation was no smoother. Dana's lungs kept filling up with fluid. When this happened, it required an in-patient procedure called pleurocentesis to remove the fluid accumulating in the pleura, the lining of the lung. Dana had a new cardiologist at Columbia, Dr. Mark Friedman, whom she adored. However, within a year, Dr. Friedman left Columbia Presbyterian to be the chief of Pediatric Cardiology at Schneider Children's Hospital on Long Island, so this resulted in a much longer car ride for us. Still, Dana wanted to remain his patient; we had assumed we would only have to deal with the traffic on the Cross Bronx Expressway once a year for checkups. Little did we know that we would become regular commuters.

I took a leave of absence from school. Dr. Friedman thought it would be best if Dana were put on home tutoring until her body acclimated to her newly rebuilt heart. For a child who already had difficulty relating to her peers, this new development was devastating. Her friends would visit occasionally, but with each visit, fewer and fewer girls came. The visits became more and more awkward. The girls gossiped about the social events that were happening at school. They talked about which teachers were wonderful and fun and which ones were boring or mean. Dana was not a part of any of this. Her teachers came to the house, one for each subject. She could not add anything of interest to their conversations; the visits merely alienated her more.

Television and books were Dana's life savers. Escaping into them distracted her from pain and boredom, both in the hospital and when she was home recuperating from her many procedures. It wasn't long before she began to sink deeper into the imaginary worlds of the television characters and become even more out of touch with the real kids at school. Those kids rejected her. Instead, she laughed with the television friends and obsessed over the intricacies of their relationships. The girls at school worried about homework, gossip, and boys; Dana worried about having fluid in her lungs. They worried about being asked to the latest party; Dana worried about going into congestive heart failure. They worried about being asked on a date; Dana worried about dying.

In addition to life-saving surgery, Dana's twelfth year was marked by one more milestone: Dana's bat mitzvah. This Jewish rite of passage, a bar or bat mitzvah, is the culmination of years of after-school study in Hebrew and consists of a religious service that signifies the coming of age of a young person. After the ceremony, the young person is considered an adult in the eyes of the Jewish community and a celebration follows.

Dana's bat mitzvah was scheduled for early December. For us, the repeat hospitalizations after our return from Minnesota in September, October, and November made it extremely unclear whether Dana would be able to even show up at the temple, much less be capable of studying for the rigorous training that was part of the preparation. But Dr. Friedman was optimistic. "This will happen," he predicted. "Get her ready and call the caterer."

The Landmark, our chosen banquet hall, graciously offered to return our deposit if need be. The temple was also very accommodating and sent the cantor or Rabbi Block to our home on the days that Dana did not feel well enough to go out. They taught her the portion of the Torah, the first five books of the Hebrew bible, from which Dana would need to read for her ceremony. The plans for the party were progressing, our dresses were purchased, and the invitations were in the mail. Relatives and friends of the family were coming from as far away as California and Florida. Dana invited the handful of friends who had proven themselves loyal while she was still being tutored at home and the few friends that she still clung to from early childhood in Fort Lee. However, in mid-November, she was still spending many days in and out of the hospital and I was getting very, very nervous. She had to have yet another pleurocentesis procedure the final week of November – just days before the celebration. Thankfully, Dr. Friedman was correct. After that trip to the hospital, the fluid never returned to her lungs.

On December 4th, one hundred and fifty relatives and friends gathered in Temple Sinai for Dana's rite of passage. Dana's tenacity and poise were evident as she stood in front of the ark which housed the Torah. She read without error in a voice that was strong and sweet. When she cradled the Torah in her arms and proceeded up and down the aisles of the sanctuary, the guests jostled each other to reach out — not to kiss the Torah, which was customary, but to kiss Dana. Her voice was strong and loud as she sang out the prayers for the bread and wine, and the congregation whispered the "amens" between sniffles. This was no longer a coming-of-age ceremony; it was a celebration of a life for someone who had bravely persevered against cruel and unfair odds.

The celebration that followed was raucous. Not a soul at the party took for granted what they had just experienced. At the typical Bat Mitzvah celebration of the time, each family member's entrance into the party was announced with a song that fit the occasion. Steve and I walked out first, followed by Jackie. When Dana's entry was announced, the band leader belted out the song "Forever Young." The lyrics seemed especially apt and poignant in that they express the hope that the child will always maintain a youthful outlook and remain courageous and strong. Before the singer could finish the refrain, all in attendance stood and sang out loudly: "May you stay forever young."

We all danced and drank with wild abandon. Dana was hoisted aloft on a chair, as was customary, and the crowd swirled around her. Jackie was lifted above the crowd next, followed by Steve and then me. A conga line snaked around the dance floor with a maraca-shaking Dana leading the dance. Steve's Sigma Alpha Mu fraternity brothers from Rutgers held onto each other's shoulders and danced in a circle to "Shout" by the Isley Brothers. They wound up on the floor, kicking their feet in the air in a dance called "The Bug." The crowd roared in laughter at these middle-aged men behaving like they were at a 1960s fraternity party.

As opposed to the cold wasteland of Dana's school, this place and these people created an oasis of love and acceptance and wrapped Dana in it, safe and warm.

Back to Reality

By January of 1989, Dana had returned to school. She had fantasized that after the Fontan surgery, every problem that she had suffered would magically be gone. It was something she'd told herself to gain the courage to undergo the surgery in the first place. "It'll all be worth it," she imagined. She thought that when she got back to school, everyone would line up outside of the house to see her. She assumed that she would be able to take gym and become a champion athlete. She hoped that she would be invited to all the parties and be able to get up and dance with everyone else.

Unfortunately, that wasn't Dana's reality. The Fontan had made her condition better, but she was still not able to exert herself the way a healthy teenager could. The lines outside the house never formed, and the athletic trophies were not forthcoming. Her heart had been fixed as best as was medically possible at that time; now my heart was breaking, watching her sit on the couch Saturday night after Saturday night, all by herself.

When I was pregnant with Dana, I worried about all the health catastrophes that could affect my baby, but never once did I worry about her having friends. Middle school plodded along for Dana, but it wasn't what she had hoped it would be. She had a few friends here and there who would invite her to the occasional movie or birthday party, but otherwise Dana seemed resigned to life as a loner.

One autumn afternoon, I heard cars honking from the distant parts of our town. The sound of horns kept getting closer until finally, dozens of cars were speeding up our block honking wildly. I looked out the window and saw that the cars contained laughing, screaming teenagers who were hanging out of the car windows shouting and shaking black and orange pom poms. There were orange and black flags with the football team's logo flapping in the wind. Obviously, the home team had won the game.

It brought me back to my own teen years when I had been a cheerleader. Being chosen as a high school freshman for the varsity squad had been a big deal at the time. Proficiency in gymnastics was a requirement, and, socially, a place on the varsity cheering team was considered a major plus. It was a guaranteed place of prominence in the hierarchical high school social world of 1962. It had all seemed so easy; I got along well with everyone, just like Jackie, who — with her funny personality — is the "cheerer upper" of our family. It never occurred to me that having friends was anything other than a natural manifestation of living.

In stark contrast to Dana, Jackie was popular, friendly, and well-liked by all. She was athletic, so was chosen first when teams were being formed. She was invited to all of the birthday parties and spent many a Saturday night sleeping over at the homes of various friends. However, she felt guilty that she had a busy social life and Dana did not. Unlike others, Dana was not enamored of this adorable, blonde sister of hers, and she made no secret of her resentment. Although they did play beautifully together some of the time, especially with their suitcase of over twenty Barbie Dolls, Dana started to bully her little sister. She refused to share or even show common courtesy toward her. She was the Boss of the Barbies and Ruler of the Remote Control. It tore at my insides to see this happening. Even though I intervened, I was not always around when they played in the basement or in one of their rooms. I could see that Dana was suffering social abuse each day, and, then, turning it around on her sister. I think part of her need to boss Jackie around stemmed from a deep desire to exert some control over a life that in too many negative ways controlled her.

When Jackie was a teenager, she told me that she accepted Dana's mistreatment because she thought Dana needed to be mean to someone and that was the one thing Jackie could do for her. My stomach dropped and my throat tightened upon hearing that. My heart broke for Dana, and I was consumed with guilt that Jackie had taken on such a burden.

One day, at a routine visit to the pediatrician, I saw a pamphlet advertising Camp Open Hearts, a camp specifically for children with congenital heart defects. It was started by a philanthropist and set up on his huge property in the Berkshires, in Massachusetts. A scar was the only requirement for admission, and the tuition for two weeks was free. I was ecstatic. Finally, a haven for Dana — a place where she could be in the country and do all the normal camp activities with other children who were as limited as she was. I imagined that this would be a euphoric experience for Dana to be able to be around children who understood. But we soon discovered that although the other kids had all had a congenital heart defect, their hearts had all been "corrected." Now, they could run, swim, hop, and jump without becoming breathless. She still enjoyed the girls in her bunk and had fun at the evening activities, but during the day Dana was still unable to participate in the activities. Even at Camp Open Hearts, she spent her time watching life on the sidelines.

The following summer, after researching camps and interviewing owners, we sent her to Camp Oquago in Andes, New York. This camp was a typical sleep-away camp but did not seem to stress athletics the way other camps did. Also, my friend, Cindy, had gone to this camp as a child and the fact that it was still in operation made me confident that they must be doing something right! The owners had promised us that they would adapt many of the activities to Dana's limitations. Sadly, once again, the experience was a disappointment. Not only did they not offer alternative activities, but the bunk counselors were not equipped to deal with the bullying heaped on Dana by her bunkmates. Bunk life was horrific for her, but we kept getting mixed messages. On each weekly phone call, she would complain about this one or that one, but her letters talked of how much fun she was having. The camp sent photos of a smiling Dana. She was even willing to return to this camp, especially when her friend, Josh, accompanied her. But, we were unaware of the stories of the bullying and Dana did not tell us until a few years later.

Pay It Forward

Sometimes transformative events happen at just the right time. Steve had a patient named Fran Kazui who had come to see him for a surgical procedure. Before he began, he chatted with her. They shared some personal information about their backgrounds and difficulties in their lives, and Steve mentioned Dana's health crises. Fran told him that she was a writer and film director. Her latest film was to be entitled "Buffy the Vampire Slayer," and it starred, among other luminaries, Luke Perry — the heartthrob of the show, "Beverly Hills 90210," which had come out in 1990 and quickly became a hit. It was 1992, and Jackie and Dana were obsessed with the show. Steve told Fran how much his kids loved Luke Perry. It turned out that she would be filming a crowd scene for the movie during the kids' upcoming school break in April and offered to put them into a scene to be filmed on Hollywood Boulevard.

Their suitcases were packed days before our flight to Los Angeles. We stayed with Steve's brother and sister-in-law, Michael and Susann. Each night we drove to the set where Buffy was filming. One thing we learned about film-making was how to hurry up and wait. Each scene could be shot five, ten, or fifty more times before the director is satisfied. There is a lot of down time and hanging around, waiting for the scene to be set. For my kids, this time was not wasted. Pee Wee Herman cracked jokes. Hillary Swank braided Jackie's hair, and Dana sat on Kristy Swanson's lap and talked quietly.

Finally, it was time for Dana and Jackie's big closeup. In their scene, Luke Perry's character rides down the escalator in an outdoor mall while talking with David Arquette's character. Dana and Jackie were riding directly behind them. There are many labor laws governing child actors, but because they had no speaking parts and were merely standing behind the performers, Fran was able to skirt around those rules. She just plopped them into the scene! They must have ridden that escalator twenty times until the scene was to Fran's liking and she called, "Cut."

This small act of kindness had a huge, positive impact on both Dana and Jackie. To say that they felt special would have been the understatement of the century. Fran provided an opportunity that created happy memories, which resonated throughout Dana's and Jackie's lives. We took millions of pictures, but the one of Luke Perry with his arms around each girl stands out in my mind. The brightness of Dana's smile was only enhanced by the light glinting off her braces. Jackie's smile screamed, "EEEEEEEEE"!

During one of the many breaks in the filming, I noticed Dana looking around at the cameras, props, and costumes. She took in the nighttime scene — scores of fans lining Hollywood Blvd, screaming for autographs. She looked at Luke Perry and the other actors rehearsing their lines. The expression on her face said, "Pinch me!" I was standing next to Fran when I heard Dana ask her, "Why are you doing this for me?" Fran replied, "Because I can, and one day you'll turn around and do something for someone else and pay it forward."

We were all invited to the New York opening of "Buffy the Vampire Slayer." We brought an entourage of relatives and friends with us. When the escalator scene came on the screen, our hooting and howling drowned out the dialogue. Two photos of Luke Perry with Dana and Jackie were blown up to poster size and mounted on Styrofoam. Those posters hung on their walls for years and still live in the basement with the bat mitzvah sign-in boards, Barbie dolls, and other childhood memorabilia.

Years later, when 21-year-old Dana was still a patient in the pediatric cardiac clinic, we were waiting to see one of the cardiologists when Dana noticed a young girl of six or seven crying hysterically. A nurse was trying to cajole her into the examination room in preparation for a cardiac catheterization, but the child clung to her mother screaming, "No cath! No cath!"

Dana walked over and asked if she could speak to the little girl. She took the little girl's hand. "I've had tons of these, see?" She pulled the neck of her sweater lower to reveal her scar. Quietly, Dana told the child exactly what would happen in the cath lab. "First, they will put in an IV. It will pinch a little but that only lasts a second or two." The child stopped sobbing, listening intently, especially after she saw Dana's scar. "That will be the worst part, everything after that will happen when you are fast asleep. And the best part," Dana continued, "is when you wake up — Mommy and Daddy will be standing right by your side."

The nurse then asked the little girl if she was ready. Dana gave her a hug, and the child took the nurse's hand and bravely walked into the catheterization lab.

We found out over the years just how much, in her own modest way, Dana had paid it forward, giving to her friends, colleagues, and students the wisdom and empathy she had gained from the difficulties in her life. She probably did not label it as such, but Dana performed many a mitzvah, the Hebrew word for good deed. It cost her nothing. Fran Kazui did a mitzvah. It cost her nothing. She gave two young girls an experience that would never be forgotten.

As Winnie the Pooh once said: "The smallest things take up the most room in your heart."

Wonderland

When Dana was fifteen, her pediatrician diagnosed her with scoliosis. Her back was curving unnaturally and if it were not corrected, she would, eventually, have difficulty breathing. I could not help but think of the cruel irony. Dana's back was literally bending from the crushing weight of the emotional burden she had to bear.

Dana needed surgery to insert Harrington Rods, which were designed to straighten the spine. We were told she would be in the hospital for one or two weeks, and that it would be a relatively easy surgery. We felt safer having the surgery done at the Mayo Clinic, just in case. If there was a cardiac-related problem, her surgeon would be right there to assist. We made plans to return to Mayo for the surgery in mid-August 1991.

After a few unhappy years at Camp Oquago, Dana had researched and found a new camp called Buck's Rock Performing and Creative Arts Camp in New Milford, Connecticut. We arranged for her to attend that summer.

This camp was made for her. Activities were available in areas that ranged from theater, art, sewing, and music to gardening, horseback riding, and even glass blowing. Campers chose the activity that most interested them on a given day and they spent as much or as little time there as they wanted. Dana loved it there and convinced Josh to attend also so they could still spend the summer together. She indulged her desire to act and was cast in the camp's production of "The Crucible." That play marked the beginning of her participation in the drama productions in high school, which continued during her years at college, acting with the Oxford Street Players at Lesley University. She spent hours at the sewing shed and developed her skill in making costumes for the shows she was in. Unfortunately, even the new friendships, camaraderie, and activities could not distract her from the fear of the upcoming scoliosis surgery in August. She decided to leave camp early and wait out the few remaining weeks before the surgical date at home.

Towards the end of August, we flew back to the Mayo Clinic for Dana's surgery. A Nestle's Crunch bar was packed in my suitcase. The surgery went so smoothly that after only a week, Steve had already flown home and Jackie was flown back to her camp, Crane Lake, which she had been attending in the Berkshires. I stayed with Dana for the few remaining days of her recovery, and planned to fly home with her that upcoming Friday. On Tuesday of that week, a nurse came in to perform the routine procedure of removing the central venous pressure line, a tube that was inserted before surgery and removed when it was no longer needed. I watched as the nurse swabbed her neck with betadine, an antiseptic to cleanse the skin. Inexplicably, I had an ominous feeling as the nurse cleansed and sterilized the site, and then removed the tube. Just like that, the procedure was over. The nurse snipped off the tip of the tube and, as is customary, sent it off to the lab to be cultured.

The following day, the doctor told me that fifteen colonies of the bacteria Staph Aureus were present on the C.V.P. line.

"What does that mean?" I asked.

"Oh, it is really nothing. The body's own immune system can deal with that," he said.

I was not happy. I had learned in seventh-grade biology that one cell becomes two and two become four. I wanted to know why the doctors had not ordered an antibiotic.

"It's not necessary," they said, but I was not assuaged.

The more questions I asked, the more doctors were sent in to placate me. On the Thursday before discharge, Dana spiked a fever. I demanded attention. I told every resident, doctor, and nurse who examined Dana that her C.V.P. line had been infected with Staph Aureus. The fever was belittled, and the fact that a virus had been going around the ICU was given as the likely explanation. I felt like I had fallen into a strange, unknown place where the normal world seemed upside down, just as it seemed to Alice when she arrived in Wonderland. Was this really the same Mayo Clinic, the medical mecca that had previously set the gold standard for the way we evaluated every other hospital? I knew I had to get Dana out of Mayo and home to Dr. Freidman, quickly.

When Friday morning arrived, I did not need a thermometer to tell me that Dana had a fever. I pumped her up with Tylenol, so that when the nurse came around to discharge her, she would not have a fever. Dana's attending orthopedist had told me previously that if Dana did have a staph infection, she would be much sicker and would have to remain at Mayo on intravenous antibiotics for six months. He said it as if it were a threat. They kept insisting her fever was being caused by a virus, but I sensed something amiss; I knew Dana needed to be where she would get better care.

By the time we were discharged and arrived at the airport, Dana was shivering. The flight attendants on the plane became our personal nurses. Luckily, the plane was not full. They were able to space everyone else out so Dana could have the three seats to herself and I could be across the aisle. I have never seen anyone get so sick so quickly. She was deteriorating before my very eyes. Nothing could keep her warm. Her teeth chattered so intensely you could hear them above the din of the jet's engine. We landed at Newark and Steve came running to greet us. In the days before cell phones, there was no call to alert him to the seriousness of Dana's condition. As soon as he saw my face, the color drained from his own. We went directly from the airport to Schneider Children's Hospital on Long Island.

Once there, her fever was 105 degrees. They cultured her blood, but I knew what it was. She was given I.V. antibiotics immediately and a few days later, the cultures came back: Staph Aureus. At this point, the infection had galloped through her entire body causing her organs to begin to fail. Her capillaries were leaking, and she required blood transfusions. She was swollen and yellow from liver failure. After all we had been through, was this how it would end?

Jackie was back at camp. I asked Dr. Friedman if we should bring Jackie home. I expected him to tell me she'd be fine, that it wasn't that serious. Instead, he said, "You have to do what you think is best." By the end of the week, we had arranged for Jackie to fly home with our cousin, Elaine, whose daughter was at camp with Jackie. Then miraculously — and to the surprise of all the myriad doctors in the ICU — Dana began to exhibit small signs of improvement. I took another leave of absence from school, which was just beginning, and sat vigil by Dana's bedside in the ICU. She had been strafed by this bullet, not killed. She suffered residual damage, however. Endocarditis, an inflammation of the heart's lining, left her already fragile heart even weaker. Unlike the threat of six months at Mayo, after three months in the ICU. in Long Island, Dana came home with a portable IV antibiotic, on which she would remain for another six months. It was so user-friendly that even Jackie could administer the antibiotic, if needed.

We were so focused on Dana's recovery from the infection, we had almost forgotten what caused it in the first place: being hospitalized for her scoliosis surgery. She was supposed to have worn a body brace to correct an additional type of curvature called kyphosis, which could not be corrected surgically but she was too uncomfortable in bed to have to wear a brace. After another month at home, Dana finally went back to school. It was the beginning of January, and she was entering her freshman year of high school. She had to wear a boxy brace all day, which barely fit under her shirt. She also had a portable IV dangling from her arm. If her classmates needed more reasons to consider Dana different, could two more devilishly cruel ones be imagined? A month later, an examination of Dana's spine revealed that the brace was not correcting the kyphosis.

Her curvature would now be permanent.

Why Do Homework?

Not surprisingly, Dana's grades were very erratic. In English and writing she excelled, but in math and science she did not. She put in very little effort to bring up her lower grades and only a moderate amount of effort into the classes in which she did well. Luckily, she had an aptitude for some classes and was blessed with a good memory. This was a constant source of aggravation for me, a teacher who expected my own students to put forth their best efforts. I battled with recalcitrant students all day long and then came home to one.

During one of our more raucous arguments, Dana lashed out at me with a question that must have been festering inside her for years. "Why should I bother with homework? I am not going to live anyway." I stood there frozen, as if I were stuck to the kitchen floor. With all that Dana had endured in her short life, she had every reason to want the answer to that question. When she was a baby, Dr. Kenert would give us estimations of what her life span could be. Each time that we saw a cardiologist, the estimate was increased from two years, when she was five months old, to eight years, to her mid-teens. Then, at some point, since she had bounced back and stabilized after each setback, the doctors stopped making predictions. Those words that Dr. Kenert said so long ago reverberated in my head. Her prognosis was still, "When she needs something, there will be something." We were still learning how to live by those words. So, when Dana hurled that question at me, I was ready for it. "Yes, you could die," I said. "But what if you don't? Then, what?" I told Dana to live each day with the belief that she will have a future. After all, we had not expected her to live this long, and, yet here she was, whining and complaining like a typical teenager. The previous month, a mother from our town was driving her daughter to the mall to purchase a dress for her upcoming prom when their car was hit from behind by a truck and both were killed. A friend's nephew, president of his class, recently accepted into the college of his choice, and showing no signs of depression, was found hanging in the garage when his mother returned from work. These and stories like these exemplified the fragility and tenuousness of life. We humans do not know when our time is up.

At the age of fifteen, her future was almost upon her. We knew that her life would have potholes and boulders in the road ahead. We also knew that we, along with her doctors, would need to be there always to get her back on the road again. It was the only way to move forward. We knew it would not be easy, but we did not know any other way.

To be truly prepared for the future, you must do your homework.

Gods of Dana's Destiny

Three more years passed, and amazingly, it was time for Dana to graduate high school. The family gathered for the ceremony and festivities that would follow. Although Dana did not win any awards for sports or academic honors, she was the recipient of the Marie Donovan Personal Achievement Award, named for a beloved teacher who had passed away several years before. This award was given to the student who had overcome the most difficulty yet still managed to persevere and succeed. To us, it was the most valuable award she could have received because it acknowledged all that she had endured but still prevailed.

Dana was accepted to Emerson College, in Boston, and in September we packed the Pathfinder and moved her into the dorm on Tremont Street. After difficulty with her first roommate, she had moved in with a new roommate, whom she loved. Dana was majoring in television production and loving school. Then, during the second semester, at the end of March, Dana called me to say that she had felt some fluttering and irregular heartbeats. Her roommate took her to Boston Children's Hospital as a precaution, where she was admitted for testing. I left my school immediately, packed a bag for a few days, and drove to Boston.

What I thought would be a few days turned into six weeks. I stayed with my cousins Jay and Nancy Lee and commuted from Newton to Boston each day. Each test revealed new information and the conclusion was that Dana's valve was defective. She would need another surgery to replace her damaged valve with a mechanical one. The damage had been caused by the endocarditis she had suffered from the Staph Aureus infection three years before as a result of the scoliosis surgery.

Dana had to leave school before she could finish her freshman year. I cannot imagine how Dana coped. When she was finally discharged from the hospital, we packed up her belongings, and Dana said goodbye to her roommate, friends, and professors. We were both heartbroken. We had moved her into the dorm with such high hopes. Would nothing ever go her way? I felt the wrath of the "Gods of Dana's Destiny." We were fighting against a cruel and unfair fate. I had dared to hope for a normal future for my daughter, and now fate had caught up with us. I indulged in some rare self-pity, and then I worked diligently to get over myself and focus on what would be our third visit to the Mayo Clinic. We chose to return there to have Dr. Dennison perform the valve replacement. Even though the orthopedic surgeon had not taken the staph infection seriously, we trusted Dr. Dennison and we believed he would give her the best chance at success.

The valve replacement surgery went very well, and we were home in less than two weeks. A mechanical valve was implanted. Aside from the tic-toc of the valve that could be heard in a quiet room — and made Dana feel like the crocodile in Peter Pan — we thought we were on the road to recovery and after the summer, expected that she would return to Emerson for the fall semester. But, before the first week home was out, she was back in the hospital on Long Island in congestive heart failure. The pleural effusion — when her lungs filled with fluid — caused difficulty breathing, and the accumulation of fluid in her abdomen, or ascites, caused her to swell so much that she looked nine months pregnant. She would then have to be admitted for the fluid to be drained from her lungs in a procedure called thoracentesis, or drained from her abdomen in a procedure called paracentesis. She was in the hospital every few weeks, but at least she felt well in the interim. Dr. Friedman thought the heart just needed time to acclimate to the new valve. We hoped he was correct.

In late October, Dana felt well enough to enjoy some frivolous trick-or-treating with a few of her high school friends who were home from college for the weekend. She dressed as Raggedy Ann. They rang the bell of our neighbor, who had been Dana's pediatrician years before. This doctor knew Dana well and was aware of her cardiac issues since his office was periodically contacted to keep them abreast of her medical progress. Dr. Shatz certainly understood the significance of abdominal swelling, but must have somehow forgotten about Dana's most recent hospitalizations. When he saw Dana in her costume, he reprimanded, "Dana! I do not think a pregnant Raggedy Ann is humorous." Dana was stunned into silence. Of all people, Dana thought her pediatrician should have known better. The ignorance was painful.

Dana spent the next year and a half going from the couch to

the hospital. When she felt well enough, Steve, Jackie, Dana, and I would go out to a local restaurant for dinner. Sometimes we would bring a friend of Dana's; other times we'd be accompanied by a variety of relatives. One evening, the waitress at Bacci asked us for our orders. She smiled sweetly at Dana and asked her when the baby was due. Everyone gasped. The tension was palpable. "I am not pregnant," Dana replied calmly. "I have a medical condition." How did she have the strength, poise, and presence of mind to respond that way? I would have been mortified. It made me realize how different our experiences have been. I know how isolated from my family and friends I felt when Dana was first diagnosed. I felt the only people who understood were those other mothers and fathers in the waiting room. I was sure that Dana felt the same, that the only ones who could understand her were those who had grown up with chronic illness as she had.

As a child, I had to deal with the effects of my parents' divorce. I fought with my sister over whose turn it was to vacuum the living room. I worried about what I would be when I grew up, but I never doubted that I would grow up. I felt desperate to know what Dana was feeling and how she was coping. I did not know what it meant to be her; I only knew what it meant to be her mother.

We lost count of the hospital admissions that year. Dana despised hospital food and refused to eat it. Her repertoire of food was never very sophisticated. She disliked most foods, especially healthy ones. Part of the problem was that after the Fontan, her salt intake was severely limited. The foods that teenagers survive on — pizza and Chinese food — were verboten. She craved that forbidden seasoning. Also, her medicines changed the taste of food, a side effect I understood better, years later, when I had my own medical emergency and could no longer tolerate the taste of formerly beloved foods. The doctors accused her of being anorexic and came close to threatening her with treatment, but I knew better. When I brought homemade lasagna or chicken nuggets and Kraft Macaroni and Cheese from home, she had no problem eating.

Dana had a pact with Dr. Friedman that any procedure requiring a needle would be preceded by the application of EMLA, a cream that numbs the skin to prevent pain. He agreed that any pain that could be avoided was worth the wait of the few minutes it took for the EMLA to work its magic. Dana had become adept at evaluating who could insert an I.V. expertly and who could not. She was now an opinionated, skillful, and assertive advocate for herself.

In one emergency admission, a nurse we had never met was trying to insert an IV. This new nurse wanted Steve and me to leave the room while she readied Dana for admission. We had never been asked to leave and were not about to start now. We refused. She bristled but went about the process of inserting the IV needle. "Where is the EMLA?" Dana asked. The nurse explained that an IV insertion did not require EMLA. Dana briefly watched the nurse painfully poke around without successfully inserting the needle. Then Dana pulled her arm away and demanded a more experienced nurse complete the task.

On Yom Kippur, the Jewish Day of Atonement, Dana was still in the hospital. Instead of the family going to my sister's house, all thirty relatives descended on the hospital cafeteria. We took over one corner of the room and spread out the bagels, lox, cream cheese, whitefish salad, and chopped liver. Dana wheeled her IV pole into the huge cafeteria, as if she were entering a testimonial dinner in her honor . . . and in a way, she was. If you didn't listen to the beeping of the machine and managed to block out those who were gawking at our crowd of well-dressed revelers, you might forget where you were. We repeated this for each subsequent holiday in which Dana was hospitalized: Thanksgiving, Chanukah, and again for Dana's birthday in December. I must believe that the love and support she had from family compensated in some small way for the difficulty of her life.

New Beginning?

*D*r. Friedman had originally thought that Dana's frequent fluid buildup was her body's slow adjustment to the mechanical valve that ticked inside of her chest. But when the first year came and went without improvement, he began to re-evaluate. Now he concluded that the valve replacement done at the Mayo Clinic had been a failure. He decided to place her on the transplant list. The time we most dreaded had arrived. Just as I'd had an ominous feeling after her scoliosis surgery, this development elicited a similarly disturbing feeling. I just did not feel the time was right.

Once Dana was on the list, she had to remain in the hospital in case a heart arrived. Each day, Dana would speak to the social worker and work toward accepting what we all thought was an imminent heart transplant. She began to believe that it would provide her with a new beginning. She was sick of being sick. She had loved college and felt worse from holding her life in abeyance than she did from her physical ailments. She was ready. Steve, Jackie and I were not.

During Dana's stay on Long Island at Schneider Children's Hospital, she developed a closeness with the nurses. Because they knew how much she hated hospital food, they included her when they ordered out for dinners. She gradually began to feel better, and she even accompanied certain nurses on their rounds at night, making friends with the other young adults who were also hospitalized.

For some reason that the doctors could not explain, after a year in and out of the hospital and a few weeks on the transplant list, the valve began to function properly. Once again, seemingly out of the blue, the fluid receded and did not return. She had more energy and looked healthier than she had since the surgery. Dr. Friedman ordered a catheterization. It showed that the heart function had, indeed, improved dramatically. She was taken off the transplant list. We were elated. Dana was devastated.

The new beginning she so desperately longed for would have to wait.

When She Needs Something

In the fall, two years after her freshman year was interrupted, Dana finally returned to college. She had made the decision to transfer to Lesley College, where she could major in education, instead of returning to Emerson. Lesley, a tiny women's college at that time, was tucked into a corner of the Harvard Law School campus. The quadrangle was the size of a suburban backyard. Yet, Dana felt she fit in better than she ever had anywhere else. She made wonderful, supportive friends, joined clubs, and acted in and sewed costumes for the classic plays that were performed by the Oxford Street Players. After she finished her sophomore year, she signed up for summer school near our home to pick up credits to make up for the year that she spent in and out of the hospital. This way she would qualify as a junior in the fall.

That September, we packed the Pathfinder once again and, this time, we moved Jackie into her dorm at the University of Massachusetts at Amherst for her Freshman year of college. Now that we had both daughters in Massachusetts, Steve and I reveled in our empty nest.

In April of 2000, my 86-year-old father died. Dana drove from Cambridge to Amherst to pick up Jackie, and they came home to be with the family for the funeral. When I saw Dana, my stomach dropped. Dana always wore bright red lipstick, but even that could not camouflage the dark, dusky blue of her lips. It looked like she had been drinking grape juice; her nails were bright blue; and when she took off her shoes, her feet looked like she had been stomping grapes. While arrangements for the funeral were being made, I called Dr. Friedman and scheduled an appointment. Dr. Friedman examined her and detected an arrhythmia, an irregularity of the heartbeat. He scheduled her for a cardiac ablation, a procedure to correct malfunctioning nerves from the heart, but thankfully felt it could wait until after the semester ended in May. Dana returned to Lesley, performed in the school play, and finished her junior year of college. When she arrived home, Dana was bluer than I had ever seen her.

On a warm, spring morning in mid-May, we creeped along the Long Island Expressway on our way to the Schneider Children's Hospital for the ablation. During that procedure, Dr. Friedman would insert a catheter into the heart muscle to correct the arrhythmias. The procedure was supposed to take between forty-five minutes to an hour but we knew from experience that a myriad of issues could arise, which would delay the procedure. When 90 minutes ticked by, we did not worry. At two hours, however, we were frantic. Finally, Dr. Friedman walked into the waiting room. His usually ruddy complexion was now chalky. He had a natural way of assuaging our fears; we knew if he was not worried, we should not worry. His grim expression told us that something was very wrong. He did not bother with euphemisms. "She is in left ventricular failure. This is the end of the line. The only course of action remaining for her is a heart transplant. It's for real this time. We must list her."

Steve and I both gaped at Dr. Friedman. No one spoke. This man was telling us that our daughter had one chance left at life. Now, we had to pin our hopes on what we most dreaded. Twenty-three years ago when we were first told this news, heart transplants were not a viable option. Since that time, immunosuppressive drugs have been developed and refined. Surgical procedures were perfected. Even in the two years since she had first been listed and removed from the list, new drugs had been developed. Twenty-three years ago, Dr. Kenert, assured us, "When she needs something, there will be something." It had been our silent mantra for twenty-three years. This time I knew it was the right one. Now we were ready.

We were all ready.

Dana begged Dr. Friedman to allow her to "wait" at Schneider. It was her second home. She had been admitted so frequently that she was close with the nurses, doctors, social workers, custodians, and other frequently admitted patients, whom she called the frequent flyers. But after two weeks, it became clear that for her to move to the top of the transplant list, she would need to be at Columbia Presbyterian, where the surgery would be performed. We were going right back to where we had started. An ambulance brought her from Schneider to Columbia. I rode with her and listened to the siren scream in my ears. Steve followed behind us, and I watched out the window as other cars hurriedly changed lanes to allow our wailing ambulance to pass.

Independence Day

Once she was admitted to Columbia Presbyterian, the real waiting began. Dana was getting weaker and bluer by the day. It became a taunting possibility that after all these years, a heart might not come in time. We managed to keep our sanity by adopting a macabre sense of humor. I squinted hungrily at bike riders who were not wearing helmets. Statistically, accidents involving bicycle and motorcycle riders who are not wearing helmets are, sadly, a source of organs for transplants. I imagined the helmet-less bike riders as little beating hearts pedaling down Route 9W: heart donors on wheels. The view from Dana's hospital room looked onto the big green hulk of a building that housed the psychiatric center. One warm, sunny day in early July, there were people milling around on the roof. Dana took one look at them peering over the side and said, "Jump! Those voices in your head are real." We howled. Black humor was never so cathartic. Slowly six weeks had gone by, and, still, she waited.

It was July fourth weekend 2000. The prevailing wisdom amongst the nurses was that long weekends were "productive." Sadly, this meant that there were often fatal accidents on holidays; we dared to hope. The Fourth of July fell on a Tuesday, so most people had both Monday and Tuesday off from work. We had a steady parade of visitors: friends of ours, Dana's friends, Jackie's friends, and relatives. Despite the cheer squad, Dana's color and mood got bluer by the day. She did not want the visitors. She could not muster the energy to be cordial. The July fourth weekend was winding down, and no heart had come in.

Our friends Steven and Cindy were with us at the hospital the evening of the fourth. Before we left for the night, Dana asked for lo mein from the local Chinese restaurant. We called in the order and our friend, Steven, went down to the lobby to await the delivery. I went to the bathroom, and on my way back to Dana's room, I heard my name being called. Steve was on the phone at the nurses' station with the doctor — he had called to tell us that a heart had come in that matched Dana's blood type. A heart had come in! We flew down the hall and into Dana's room, where the nurses crowded around the bed to hear us share the good news with her. I climbed into bed with Dana and held her while we all sobbed. I could only imagine what my daughter was feeling at that moment: relief that her waiting was over; joy that an opportunity for a new life was finally at hand; unspeakable grief that someone else, a total stranger, needed to die to make her new beginning possible. While we rejoiced, another family mourned. We felt hope, sorrow, guilt, and fear all at once. During the commotion, Steven walked into the room with lo mein. Cindy, who had been in a corner of the room watching all of this unfold in silence, blurted out, "I feel like I'm in someone else's movie!" As the motto goes, hurry up and wait. And then hurry up and wait some more.

We had waited for twenty-three years, and now we needed

to act fast. Dana was given an injection of steroids to begin the process of turning off her immune system. We needed to pick up Jackie at home and bring her back to the hospital, along with books, toothbrushes, and other accouterments we would need while waiting out the surgery. Steven and Cindy drove me home while Steve waited back at the hospital with Dana. The George Washington Bridge was lit up in honor of the new millennium, and as the car sped west Macy's fireworks bounced off the Hudson River and lit up the sky. While the nation celebrated its birthday, we anticipated our daughter's rebirth.

Once home, I called my cousin Lori to go to my mother's house and break the news to her that a heart had come in. I didn't want her to be alone to hear this news about her granddaughter. Then, I ran around the house with a shopping bag over my arm, swiping razors, magazines, and fruit from the refrigerator. I had my cell phone in one ear and the portable house phone in the other. Jackie and I looked like the Keystone Cops, bumping into one another on our race around the house to get what we needed and return to the hospital for the vigil. Passing at breakneck speed through the kitchen, I saw the blur of Steven and Cindy out of my peripheral vision, sitting at the kitchen table wolfing down the lo mein.

They dropped us off back at the hospital. Jackie and I pushed the elevator button ten times in our haste to get to Dana's room. We knew it would be hours before they would be ready to take her for the surgery, but time seemed to compress, and we became irrational in our fear that we would not make it to her room in time to say goodbye.

Jackie crawled into bed with Dana and me while watching

the movie, "A Bug's Life." Steve was sprawled in the lounge chair with his feet propped up on the bed. We seemed to have compressed ourselves into the space allotted in the twin sized hospital bed. We were one organism; a tangle of legs, arms and feet, blonde hair entangled in red. You could not tell where one of us left off and the other began.

At five a.m., an orderly arrived with a narrow gurney. Then, we took the long walk alongside Dana to the operating room. We had done this walk before, too many times to count. Each time, however, I felt as though there should be a clergyman in the front of the procession reading from a bible like a prisoner on his last walk to the electric chair. I was optimistic, but all too aware of the reality. Dana would go into the operating room, but would she come out?

Weeks before, Jackie had asked Dr. Friedman what Dana's prognosis would be. She told him that she wanted the truth. He said that Dana's odds of making it through the surgery were not good. Because of all the previous surgeries, there was an abundance of scar tissue to navigate around surgically. His fear was that they might not be able to control the bleeding. The surgeon had told Steve and me the same information, and, yet, we had to believe she would make it. She was our Energizer Bunny, a survivor who kept going against all odds. Who survives a virulent staph infection? Not many. Who is taken off the transplant list? Not many. When she needs something there will be something . . .

Once again, we squirreled into a quiet corner of the waiting room. We had done this before, but, this time, we did not have a retinue of relatives. We did not want to have to speak; we did not want to have to console anyone else. I was grateful that my father had died the previous April because he would not have honored our wish to wait at home.

After the first hour, we found an empty room and told the administrator at the nurses' station where we could be found. We were used to periodic updates about the progress of the surgery from Dana's many surgeries at the Mayo Clinic; at Columbia, no updates were forthcoming. One hour turned to two, then four, then eight. No one came to report any news. I spent hours staring out of the window in our waiting room and watched the cars and buses below. We kept the old adage, "No news is good news," in our heads, afraid to go to the nurses' station and find out if we were right. Finally, on my way back from the soda machine, in the tenth hour, I stopped to ask the nurses if they had heard any news. They said they had been looking for us all afternoon but couldn't find us; the administrator who knew our whereabouts had gone off duty and didn't bother to let anyone know where we were. The nurse relayed our whereabouts to the O.R. so that as soon as the surgeon was done, he could locate us.

After twelve hours of surgery, Dr. Mosca, the transplant surgeon, walked into our private waiting room and flopped on the plastic couch. He swiped his surgical cap from his head and said: "She's done. It was a bloody mess, but she has a new, young heart beating inside her and she is pink." He stood up and I threw my arms around him.

There are strict rules about the privacy of the heart donor.

Dana and I each wrote separate letters of gratitude to the donor family. These letters were delivered to the family through the hospital. We put our names and return address on our letters so that if the family wanted to contact us they could. Within weeks we received a response with photographs from the family. The donor was a red-headed girl only a few years younger than Dana. She had been in the pool alone practicing for her up-coming swim meet. When she was found, she was unconscious. When the doctors removed her from life support, the family made the excruciatingly difficult decision to donate her organs. As a result of one family's horrific tragedy, seven other people, including Dana, were given the gift of life.

Changing of the Guard

The road to recovery after the transplant was easier than we expected. For the first three months after the transplant, Dana required a weekly heart biopsy to test the heart tissue for signs of rejection. A catheter was inserted into her neck and snaked down into her heart, at which point a snip of tissue was taken and biopsied. Her neck looked like she had been cavorting with vampires.

Adjusting to the new heart created other unexpected problems, which took their emotional toll on Dana. The steroids and immunosuppressive drugs keeping her new heart from being rejected by her body caused horrendous side effects. Aside from other medical problems, what bothered Dana most of all was the weight she put on and the swelling in her face, a condition called Cushing Syndrome. Almost immediately, her face became very full and round; this is referred to colloquially as "moon face." She was upset each time she looked in the mirror. In addition, the texture of her hair became thick and dry compared to the lustrous, red hair she had before the transplant. Fortunately, as the levels of the drugs were reduced over time, the worst of these effects from the steroids diminished.

I was off from school for the summer and could take Dana to her appointments and biopsies as needed. By October, the biopsies were reduced to once every six months. The new transplant cardiologists felt she would be ready to resume college by January.

Along with Dana's new heart came a new set of doctors. Dr.Friedman, whom she adored, was a pediatric cardiologist, not a cardiac transplant specialist, so he could no longer be her physician. Miraculously, he had kept her alive until this moment, and now she had to shift her trust to a team of strangers. It would not be easy to duplicate the relationship she had with him. He understood her fears and complaints. He laughed at her jokes and admonished her predilection for a high-salt, junk-food diet with humor. "No 'ito' foods," he had scolded. "No foods that end in i, t, o: No Burrito. No Cheetos. No Doritos." He teased her in a way that validated her needs and yet still hammered home the message that her eating habits could be harmful. At twenty-three years old, she knew it was only a matter of time before she had to switch to an adult cardiologist anyway. In more ways than one it was time to move on.

Jackie's Turn

Jackie had always been the obedient child, the one who did as she was told. When Dana was in the hospital for months on end, Jackie adjusted to having only one parent home in the early evening, while the other went from work to the hospital to be with Dana. On the weekends, Jackie brought her school books and studied in the chair next to Dana's bed doing whatever homework she had as best she could amid the whirring and beeping of cardiac telemetry machines.

When one spends as much time in a hospital as our family, there are many things that happen that are frightening and upsetting. One of Dana's roommates at Schneider had a mysterious vascular disease that required her to periodically have part of one or both legs amputated. One leg had been amputated above the knee and the other above the ankle. One Saturday afternoon, Dana's roommate lifted her legs from under the covers, revealing her amputated legs. Jackie took one look and turned white. She had nightmares about this girl for months.

As Jackie got older, she spent less and less time at the hospital and was allowed to stay home alone or with a friend. She had spent a lot of time with my mother when she was young, but as she got older and did not need a babysitter, she spent a lot of time alone. She never complained. But now that Dana was doing so well, all the fears and resentments that had accumulated over the years demanded an outlet. It was Jackie's turn to finally feel all that she had been suppressing since she was old enough to know that our family was different from other families. All that was needed was a catalyst to open the door.

September 2001 was the beginning of Jackie's junior year at the University of Massachusetts and Dana's senior year at Lesley. On September 11th, two planes flew into the north and south towers of the World Trade Center in Manhattan. My school is across the Hudson River in West New York, New Jersey, overlooking the New York skyline. I watched in horror with my students from our classroom window as the second plane hit. When the buildings came down, so did Jackie's fortitude. Since the cell phone towers were destroyed, communication was cut off. Steve's office was on 57th street, miles from the towers, but as far as Jackie was concerned, New York City seemed two blocks long. She watched the black cloud of smoke and debris engulf lower Manhattan on television, and she became convinced that somehow Steve was dead. Dana and Jackie were able to communicate through Instant Messenger, but neither could reach us. It was four hours later when Jackie borrowed a friend's cell phone with a Massachusetts area code that she was finally able to reach me. By that time, Steve had been able to call my school on a landline and I knew that he was safe. He was waiting at New York Hospital to help the many wounded who were expected to flood the emergency room, but who, sadly, never materialized. Jackie wailed a pitiful "mommy" into the phone. Like all families that day, we desperately needed to be together and see for ourselves that we were each okay.

As the days and weeks rolled on, the feeling of dread never left us. We worried every day that the George Washington Bridge would be targeted and were convinced that this would occur while Steve was commuting to or from work. He carried a hammer on the floor of the front seat of his car, in what seemed like a realistic fear that a plane would fly into the George Washington Bridge while he was on it. If his car fell into the charcoal waters of the Hudson River, he would have the hammer to break the window and escape. For over a month, every time I looked out of my classroom window, I saw the column of smoke rising from where the towers had stood, looking like two black tornados frozen in place. I had a sickening drop in my stomach each time I looked at that skyline.

Jackie responded to this constant threat viscerally. Her stomach problems, which had been dormant, came back with a vengeance. It got so bad that on many days she could not make it to classes at all. It was not until her grades came in that December that she told us what was happening.

During winter break, Jackie was put on medicine to alleviate her stomach issues, but the condition did not get better. Despite this, she insisted on returning to school for the second semester. She was supposed to have spent the semester in Florence, Italy, but the fear of being out of the country with the threat of terrorism still palpable kept her from going. She thought she would be able to handle school, but her inability to make it to classes and the constant feeling of dread was hindering her ability to concentrate and do classwork. At the same time, my mother was put on hospice care for a recurrence of chronic lymphoma. Jackie did not want to bother Steve or me with her worsening stomach problems and plummeting grades.

That June 2002, Dana graduated from college. She had completed one year at Emerson College and three at Lesley, but with all the time in between for medical issues, it took her eight years to complete her degree. We were ecstatic. She was the proverbial tortoise with red lipstick who had won the prize by plodding on slowly and steadily against great odds. We planned a small celebration in Boston with a few family members and her old friend, Josh. Dr. Friedman flew to Boston to watch Dana walk down the aisle as a graduate. Once home, we threw a large party for family and friends.

Jackie waited until the festivities for Dana were over to tell us that she had been placed on academic probation. Once again, she had put her own needs aside while Dana became the focus of our attention. When my mother died in July, Jackie was inconsolable. Steve and I felt it would be best for her to take a year off and heal before returning to school to finish her senior year. The year was miserable. Jackie's stomach issues were being managed, but we fought constantly. She was depressed and angry at Steve and me for years of what she perceived as unequal treatment, with all the focus in the family on Dana. She was right, of course, but even if we could have gone back in time to do it over, we did not know how we could have possibly done it any differently. It was an untenable situation for us all. How could we have made the need for attention equal for our daughters? I was always aware of the inequalities, but was at a loss as to what to do about them.

Years before, when Dana was at home for the staph infection, I had taken a leave of absence from school to care for her. Since I was not at school, I was supposed to see Jackie in the annual Halloween Parade at her school for the first time. We planned what she would have for lunch and what costume she would wear. The day of the parade, I was supposed to pick her up from school, for lunch, get her into her costume, and then take her back to school. I was meant to be among the stay-at-home moms cheering on the sidelines at the school parade. That morning, after Jackie left for school, Dana felt numbness and tingling along the left side of her body. I called Dr. Friedman and he told me to bring Dana in immediately for an M.R.I. He was concerned it might be a stroke. A stroke! I was frantic. But, first, I had to go to school and tell Jackie that I would not be able to be at the parade after all. Grandma Charlotte would come and pick her up, get her into her costume, and be the "parent" cheering at the parade. Her eyes filled up but she did not cry. I felt guilty and ripped in two. Years later, Jackie resurrected this story and demanded to know why her father could not have come home and taken Dana so I could have gone to the parade. She was right. It had never occurred to me.

I was reminded of our visits with Catherine MacKenzie, the social worker at the Mayo Clinic who specialized in the siblings of Mayo Clinic's pediatric patients. She warned us to pay attention, to heed the tacit demands of Jackie's need for recognition and attention. Intellectually we knew what we needed to do, but we did not know how. We struggled to balance the medical emergencies of one daughter with the everyday needs of the other, though they were just as important.

One night, during a screaming match, I tried to defend myself. At the time, I had felt that Jackie's demands were unfair. What were we supposed to do, leave Dana in a hospital by herself? Put her in a cab to her doctor's appointments? Jackie had known the solution, though she couldn't articulate it until years later. We had taken time off from school and work each time Dana had an emergency or routine doctor's appointment. I had taken months off from work when she was recuperating from the Fontan procedure and needed care at home, and once again when she was hospitalized for the staph infection. Why hadn't we taken even one day to take Jackie to the zoo? Why hadn't we taken a day off every other month or two or three to take Jackie out for something special? Why? Neither Steve nor I had an answer. We could not go back in time; all we could do was acknowledge that she was right and offer a belated and sincere apology. We all cried. The realization that we finally understood the depth of Jackie's resentment and our heartfelt remorse was the first baby step in Jackie's healing, but with two steps forward there is an inevitable step backwards. Jackie returned to school the following September to finish her senior year, but fate would not be so kind as to allow her path to proceed unimpeded.

"Gornisht Mit Gornisht"

Jackie left for Massachusetts in July 2003 and moved into her new apartment. I had finished school at the end of June and began my annual eight weeks of unemployment. I relished this time because my summer vacation was finite and precious. In my backyard, I bent down to pull a weed and felt a sharp pain in my back. Instead of this minor nuisance getting better, it got worse. I have had aches and pains from arthritis since age fifteen, but this felt different. I was in so much pain that I began to count the minutes until I could take the next dose of Advil, the only remedy that offered a slight bit of relief.

By early August, I was spiking a low-grade fever at night. During the day, except for the constant pain in my back, I felt relatively normal, if a bit tired. I found myself coming home in the afternoon and napping, something I have never done. In addition, my menopausal night sweats that had all but disappeared made a raging comeback, and each morning I woke up drenched. Steve sent me to an internist he knew at New York Hospital where he worked. The internist thought I looked great. "Gornisht mit gornisht," he had said, which translates loosely from the Yiddish as "a whole lot of nothing." And then he added, "But I don't like that fever."

He sent me to an infectious disease specialist.

Dr. Herman took blood and examined me from head to toe. I had a chest x-ray, which he put up on the viewer in his office. He looked at it and said, "There's your problem, but I don't know what it is." To my untrained eyes, it looked like my right lung harbored something that resembled a star nebula I had once seen in an eighth-grade science book.

He sent me for an MR., immediately.

I could see the radiologists reading my MRI in the glass enclosure in the back of the procedure room. When I asked for the results, no one could look at me. Finally, the tech who had administered the MRI announced, "The doctor will call you with the results." It was then that I started to worry. By the time I got home that afternoon, Steve, who had had dinner plans that evening, was pulling into the driveway behind me, his face an unhealthy shade of gray. Standing in the kitchen, he told me that he had gotten a call from Dr. Herman. The MRI revealed a malignant mass in my lung. The blood felt as if it drained from my entire body and I slid down the wall.

Jackie flew home the next day. She put her head in my lap and cried for two hours while I stared at the heating grate in the opposite wall of the den and Steve made phone calls to schedule appointments for me at Memorial Sloan Kettering Cancer Center, where he was also on the staff in the dental clinic. Steve, Dana, or Jackie accompanied me on the hospital visits for CAT scans, MRIs, gallium scans, and biopsies. After two weeks of thinking I had lung cancer, the biopsy revealed the "good" news . . .

I had Stage Four B Cell Lymphoma.

The doctors were elated. They explained that Lymphoma was much more easily treated than lung cancer. I would begin the first of two regimens of chemotherapy in early September.

When it was time for Jackie to return to school, she did not want to go. The thought of her being home, crying in my lap and seeing me lose my hair did not seem like the best plan for her or me. I thought she would be better off at school where she would have the distraction of classes and friends. I knew that I needed all the energy I had to keep myself together, and the thought of being strong for anyone else exhausted me. It was hard enough having Dana around the house. She was working as a nursery-school teacher; the role reversal of patient and caretaker did not sit well with either of us.

Steve wailed away at night crying and railing at God or fate about the cruelty and unfairness of yet another calamity in our family. Quietly, night after night, I sat listening to him bemoan our fate — but I could not be the one to console him. I could not hear his sorrow and I could not hear his anger. He had always been the rock of the family, the strong sentry at Dana's bedside. Now, I needed him to be the stalwart soldier at my side. It was not his turn to fall apart, and, although I had no intention of drowning, I needed him to hold the oar out while I treaded through the uncharted, turbulent waters of chemo. I finally had to set some boundaries. "You have a brother. You have a business partner. You have friends. Open up to them," I screamed, my words like a pail of cold water thrown in his face. "I cannot bear to hear this night after night." Each sob of his was like the Jewish burial practice of shoveling dirt, not over my coffin, but over my ability to believe I would live.

He never cried in front of me again.

After the initial shock of diagnosis, Steve became the brace that held me up. I obsessed over the plight of other men or women less fortunate than I who had to deal with the debilitating effects of cancer, but had no decent health insurance, no one to help them with meals or housework, not even a simple ride to the doctor. The teachers at school became my personal catering service. Every other night a fully prepared meal would appear at my door. So much food came to my house that it began to feel like the scene in the Disney cartoon, "The Sorcerer's Apprentice," when the brooms dump pail after pail of water flooding the sorcerer's well. We were inundated with food. I had to ask my colleagues to deliver food only twice a week so we could have a chance to eat all the leftovers before the next platter arrived.

I experienced countless kindnesses, but certain instances stand out. My sister worried constantly, though she tried not to show it. Upon seeing me in a headscarf for the first time, she tried to get the look of sorrow off her face before I saw her and she told me that I looked beautiful. My friend Cheryl, who I have known since high school, scoured New York City for gifts that would lift my spirits and help me to feel better. Each item in the gift basket was researched and lovingly chosen. It was a month in the making and the soaps, lotions, and creams were balms that not only soothed my skin, but my psyche and soul at the same time.

My sister-in-law, Susann, who lived 3,000 miles away in Los Angeles, called me every day, her little voice with its southern Missouri accent on the phone saying, "It's meeee." She came to New Jersey to see me shortly before I started chemotherapy, and taught me how to tie a stylish scarf around my head and doll up my eyes in preparation for the hair and eyebrow loss that was yet to come. She was the one person I could talk to about my deepest fears. She gave me the permission to be down, and she didn't expect to be lifted up. Maybe the physical absence during my treatment made that possible. She did not see the worst: the IV in my arm, my green tinged skin, the sores on my lips, and the size four jeans that hung from my body. To not see is sometimes to not believe – not fully – and this advantage allowed Susann to be more upbeat than others.

Chemo began in September 2003. When Jackie came home for Thanksgiving that November, she was so shocked to see what I looked like. It sent her running for the bathroom. She had been going to classes that semester and enjoying them while she was there. However, once she got back to her apartment, the distractions were gone and she was obsessed over losing me. We should have pulled her out of school, but to say we were, once again, preoccupied would be an understatement. She squeaked through the semester with incompletes, promising to hand in the missing items before the final deadline. She did not. She could not. Looking back, it turned out that even though it was difficult for Dana to see me every day, it also made her acceptance easier. She had her finger on the pulse of how I was doing. When I felt well, she saw me having lunch with friends and running errands. Dana knew that I was coping relatively well. But Jackie hadn't seen me until I was already three months into treatment. The changes were stark. Out of sight for Jackie was not out of mind, unlike Susann who had not seen the physical transformation once I started chemo.

Midway through my chemo, I had a CAT scan. We made an appointment to learn the results. Steve and I were both anxious. I knew that if the scan showed no progress, I would have to have a bone marrow transplant. I was terrified. Dr. Seltzer asked me how I was feeling. "What are the results of the CAT scan and I'll tell you how I'm feeling," I said. He replied, "When I looked at the scan, I almost fell off the chair because your thyroid lit up like a Christmas tree. But upon closer inspection, I realized it was a separate cancer and not a metastasis of the lymphoma. That is good news." Steve and I stared at him. He continued, "The lymphoma is responding well to the treatment and the tumors are shrinking. Thyroid cancer is separate and easily treated. When you recover from the effects of chemo, you'll need to undergo surgery to have your thyroid removed." The doctors called this an "incidentaloma" because it was discovered incidentally and was not connected to the lymphoma.

We left the office, stunned and speechless.

Was this really "good" news?

Jackie fell deeper into a hole and found it impossible to sleep, much less get the schoolwork done that was required.

They Save Lives Here

I completed the first regimen of chemo called R-CHOP in mid-October. Steve had dropped me off at Memorial Sloan Kettering every other week for my six- hour out-patient infusions. At the end of the day, a friend or relative would pick me up and bring me home. After six weeks, that phase of the treatment was completed, and I began the experimental chemo protocol known by the acronym I.C.E. I would be admitted for three nights for I.V. chemo infusion every other week. For this in-patient treatment, I needed to arrive at the admitting office promptly at 7:30 AM. I knew the drill. Come early. Hurry, hurry. Hurry up and wait. So wait I did. I always wore my cozy clothes: black velour sweatpants, a black tee shirt, and matching black velour sweatshirt. I always wore it tightly zipped to protect against the perennial chill that I felt in the waiting room and everywhere else, for that matter. It seemed to me that my bones were generating the cold like a portable air conditioner. I wondered if that was why the chemo treatment I was receiving was called I.C.E.

After Steve dropped me off in front of the hospital, he got in his car and made his way back to the West Side to go to work. At the end of the day, he would trudge into my room to see with his own two eyes that I was okay. Then, once again, he would get into his car and wend his way up the East River Drive and across the bridge to go home.

On our way into the city one morning, as we neared York Avenue, we were stopped by a woman in the crosswalk whose hand was raised against our movement like a traffic cop. She motioned for us to halt, and with her other hand beckoned the children who were lined up on the sidewalk, each holding the hand of a buddy, to begin the process of crossing the street. We waited and watched as the procession of first- or second-grade children and their chaperones skipped, bounced, or lollygagged across the street. I became hysterical. I had almost forgotten my life as a teacher, it seemed so far away. It was one of the few times I had cried since receiving the diagnosis. That should be me. I wondered, would it ever be me again?

As I settled in my chair in the admitting office, I began my waiting ritual by finishing the Arts section of the *New York Times*. I then folded the paper in a way that enabled me to work on the crossword puzzle, the best relaxation and escape that I have yet to find. When I did the crossword, everyone around me disappeared. I plugged in the headphones to my iPod and allowed Joni Mitchell and Judy Collins to take me further away from the reality of the hospital. "Someday soon . . . " Judy promised.

On most mornings, there was no conversation in the waiting room. Everyone knew why the others were there. A tacit empathy was palpable. No one wanted to know the details. Privacy was respected. A quiet atmosphere prevailed, aside from the televisions droning on in each corner of the room, the sirens wailing and horns honking their way up and down York Avenue. One particular morning, however, the silence was shattered by a newcomer. He stomped in the room and announced loudly to the nurse at the admissions desk. "I have an 8:00 appointment for admission." The nurse politely took his name and asked him to have a seat. We were all aware that a bed may not become available for any of us until three, four, or even five o'clock that evening. But even though the nurse informed him of that, the newcomer did not think that information should apply to him. He sat down. Just five minutes had passed when he got up again, and loudly declared that he had an 8:00 appointment and it was now five after. We regulars looked up but said nothing. He sat down and we went back to our newspapers, music, and private thoughts. Still, the newcomer continued to fidget in his seat. He harrumphed for dramatic effect. He crossed and uncrossed his legs. He opened his newspaper and ceremoniously folded it back only to not read anything. Then he started the unfolding and refolding process all over again. I did not think paper could make so much noise.

Sure enough, within a few minutes, he was up again at the nurse's desk. She told him again that she had his information, and that he would be called when a bed was available on the appropriate floor. He flopped down loudly and started muttering to those of us sitting in the waiting room, as though we were his allies. No one engaged him. We just listened to his complaints. "It's not right!" he declared. "What kind of a place is this? My time is important. If I ran my business like this, I would be fired." He went on in that manner for a few minutes.

Some who have not been afflicted with illness harbor the erroneous conviction that illness is ennobling; that there is something to be learned from a frightening diagnosis; that people who, in health, exhibited selfish or arrogant behavior would see the error of their ways and miraculously reform their egotistical, haughty, or obnoxious personalities. I have found this to be untrue. Once, during a previous six-hour stay in the out-patient chemo lab, a gentleman who was parked next to my little cubicle spent an hour conducting business on his phone. We were only separated by a white curtain. I listened to his stentorian voice on his cell phone while he bought or sold stocks, and I listened while he berated an underling to do this and that. No one else in the infusion room said a word. Finally, when his grating voice prevented the respite of my Benadryl-induced sleep, I pressed the button for the nurse to silence him. He was incredulous and thought I was wrong for inhibiting his ability to conduct business.

In the waiting room, when the haughty newcomer sat back down for the fifth time, he was still huffing and puffing. Quietly, a tall man in brown linen pants and wearing a blue bandana gently put his newspaper on his lap. He looked up at the strident newcomer and waited until the newcomer caught his eye. Plainly, he stated, "They save lives here." He did not shout. He did not use a sarcastic tone. He just said what needed to be said, put his paper back in front of his face, and resumed reading. The entire waiting room broke out into wild applause. The newcomer did not know where to look. He was baffled and, I hope, humiliated. We regulars thought he was the most foolish man on York Avenue that morning. When the applause died down, one-by-one the regulars resumed their reading, daydreaming, and praying, and the rest of the day passed uneventfully as our names were eventually called to have our IVs inserted and to be escorted to our hospital rooms.

We didn't hear another peep from the newcomer.

Time to Heal

I completed chemo by the end of December. The drugs left my body weak, but free of the lymphoma. I felt like someone had stolen my brain and replaced it with cotton candy. I had too much trouble focusing on the road to drive a car safely anywhere except the corner supermarket. I could barely finish a sentence without forgetting what I had been talking about. My emotions intensified. But, I was grateful to be alive and indebted to all the people who had driven me to the doctor, picked up the dry cleaning, did the food shopping, and called on the phone. I was like a drunkard, whimpering words of love to all who would listen.

After a few months, I had the thyroidectomy to remove the thyroid gland. Gradually, I began regaining my strength. I once again had the strength to lift a pot of spaghetti from the stove to drain it in the sink. In mid-April, I returned to school. When I had left the previous June, my seventh-grade students said goodbye, expecting to see me in September because I was scheduled to be their teacher again for the following eighth grade year. Now, with the school year almost over, I was anxious about returning. Perhaps I should have taken the rest of the school year off to recuperate? I worried about navigating the steep stairs in the hundred-year-old school where I worked. I had left school for summer break with shoulder-length curly hair and worried about the reactions I would get when I showed up twenty pounds thinner and with a crew cut. The moment I entered, however, all of my fears were assuaged. Ancient Romans could not have greeted their emperor with more excitement. The cheers and tears were enough to dispel any misgivings I had and made me sure that I was where I belonged: back in front of my classroom.

A few months later, I was out of school for summer break. Steve and I planned a trip to Hawaii. We had been there several times before at oral surgery conventions and we decided that a trip to paradise with the kids was what we all needed to heal. We stayed at the Royal Hawaiian Hotel on Oahu for two nights and lolled on the beach sipping Pina Coladas. Then we flew to Kauii and took a ride in a helicopter over the magnificent Na Pali Coast. Steve and Dana, who are both afraid of heights, were terrified. But when we landed back on terra firma, both Steve and Dana managed to agree that the beauty of the aerial vista made the fear worth it.

Our hotel arranged for Dana and Jackie to swim with the dolphins. They didn't quite do any swimming, but they loved the experience of being in an enclosed pool petting the dolphins who were rubbing up against them. We drove all over the island in a convertible singing "Bali Hai," the song from the movie "South Pacific," about the beautiful island that can be seen from Kauii. We marveled at the beauty of Waimea Canyon. We ended our trip on the Big Island of Hawaii. Compared to the luscious green of Oahu and Kauii, the stark volcanic, moonlike landscape we encountered was a shock to the eyes. After a few days spent driving around the island's many different climate zones, we were all united in our belief that the special, strange beauty of Hawaii and the other islands was the essential medicine we all needed to heal.

Mighty Mouse

Jackie finished her second semester of junior year, but just barely. When Jackie first found out about my "good" news — thyroid cancer — she fell even deeper into a hole and found it impossible to sleep, much less get the schoolwork done that was required. We all decided it would be best for her to transfer to a school near home to finish her degree. She needed to be near us. During the semester, in addition to coping with my illnesses, her best friend's father had died suddenly of a heart attack, which only exacerbated her anxiety over the health of those she loved. Jackie's focus now turned to Steve. "Get a check-up! Get a check-up!" It was her constant refrain. In June 2005, Steve acquiesced and made an appointment for a complete physical. A sonogram revealed kidney cancer, but, fortunately, it had been detected so early that a surgical removal of the small tumor would cure him without the need for chemo or other drugs. The type of cancer he had sneaks in and does its damage over twenty years before any symptoms appear. Once they do, little can be done. The innocent check-up that Jackie insisted on revealed a ticking time bomb, hiding in plain sight. Jackie had saved his life. She was our Mighty Mouse. When trouble erupted, Mighty Mouse, the cartoon super mouse, was on the scene, the theme song blaring, "Here He Comes to Save the Day!"

Jackie enrolled in one of the smaller New Jersey state schools, Ramapo College. Living home was not exactly what she had in mind, but she needed to finish school with as few distractions as possible. With the help of a wonderful therapist, Jackie's anger and resentment found its voice. We made sure her words did not fall on deaf ears; just knowing that we heard her and understood her helped Jackie exorcize her fury.

A year later, Jackie graduated from college. We put up a tent in the yard and celebrated her achievement with friends and family. She immediately began her masters in education and started on her career in teaching. I am convinced that the difficulties she experienced growing up helped make her a compassionate and dedicated teacher who still, years later, is beloved by her students and their parents alike.

Coping Skills

I am often asked how Steve and I do it. Often, this question comes to the minds of friends or family when they experience their own medical trauma.

I have thought a lot about this question.

Sometimes I felt as though the drama in our family was happening to someone else. Each new episode snapped Steve and me out of our everyday personas, and we morphed into superhero versions of ourselves. Those characters are strong and capable of taking in detailed medical information and parsing through it rationally. They are each unflappable and unemotional. Decisions are made and dealt with in a professional manner. We focused on the here and now; we didn't have the luxury of worrying about the future.

I had realized when Dana was still a baby that having a chronically sick child meant being deprived of the joy of dreaming about the graduations and weddings that other parents took for granted. As a little girl, when Dana was asked what she wanted to be when she grew up, her answer was always the same: "I want to be a mommy." I mourned the loss of dreaming about tomorrow, and I knew that even if tomorrow came, it would not be one in which

Dana would become a mother. This process of mourning helped me gain the ability to parent a child whose future would always be in doubt with optimism. We became experts at transforming into Pragmatic Parents; when we needed to call upon those traits, the change happened automatically. as an actor who slips into a new costume to emerge on stage as a different character."

I became adept at compartmentalizing the events in my life. When Dana was awaiting a heart, first at Long Island Jewish Hospital and then at Columbia Presbyterian, I went to school each day and taught. I laughed with my colleagues and was patient with my students. I was aware of the knots in my stomach, and perhaps now and again I was quicker to snap, but if you did not know what was occurring in my life you would not have noticed anything amiss. At the end of the school day, I got into my car and drove the hour to the hospital to sit with Dana. When Steve relieved me, I would go home and help Jackie with homework and return the myriad calls I had received that day. I did what I had to do to survive.

When I was diagnosed with cancer, I wondered if it was the result of all that pent up emotion. Did it build up year after year? Did it pile up inside me like the silt in a riverbed until it finally blocked some important bodily function with the residue of unexpressed sorrow and fear? For years, I worried about my inability to cry. But, thirty-five years after Dana's diagnosis and eight years after mine, I was grateful that I could cope with all the trauma and still enjoy the relationships and enriching events in my life.

Unfortunately, life wasn't quite finished putting my abilities to the test.

Perfect Match

We were on our way to a wedding reception in Boston for my cousin Jay's son, Dan. We had Billy Joel blasting from the car radio, and Dana and I were singing along. Cell phones were now a regular part of our lives and as we sang the refrain to "Piano Man," Dana received a phone call. It was Doctor Ahmed, her wonderful adult transplant specialist, calling with the results of a previous routine blood test. Over the past few months, Dr. Ahmed was keeping a wary eye on Dana's creatinine level, an indicator of kidney function. The number had been creeping up; she called to say that the most recent blood test showed an alarmingly steep increase in her level. An appointment was scheduled for the upcoming Monday. The previously sunny and happy-go-lucky atmosphere in the car was replaced by a thick gray cloud of fear and worry. We didn't want to dampen the mood of the wedding festivities. We managed to enjoy ourselves, but the anxiety we each felt was sensed by my cousins.

We considered Jay and his wife, Nancy Lee, both physicians, to be our medical gurus. They had accompanied us to Stanford University Hospital all those years ago when we saw Dr. Johnson, and we discussed all of our medical decisions with them. We even had them named in our will to be in charge of Dana's medical care if something happened to Steve and me. They were the first ones we called after we saw the kidney specialist on Monday.

A series of tests revealed that Dana's kidneys were failing. If she could receive a kidney transplant within the next few months, she would be able to avoid dialysis. Unlike other organs, a kidney can be received from a living donor. My lymphoma made me an unacceptable donor. Steve's kidney cancer disqualified him, too. Donors do not need to be blood relatives, so it is not uncommon to hear of a friend or a total stranger donating a kidney to one in need. We could not bring ourselves to ask people if they would consider donating an organ to our child. This is a favor that cannot be asked lightly. I really do not know how I would have responded if the circumstances were reversed and I was asked to donate my kidney to someone else's child.

Nevertheless, my niece, Debbie, my husband's brother, Michael, and his sister, Randy, all came forward to be tested as possible matches for donation. Most surprising, Jorge, a former student of mine with whom I had become very close, also asked to be tested. Most distressing, however, was Jackie's desire to be tested. Could I allow both of my children to undergo surgery? Ethically, if Jackie had been under eighteen, we would have carried the burden as her parents for making the decision. But Jackie was an adult, and she was adamant.

The testing for donor compatibility seeks twelve matching markers in the blood. An organ is considered viable if there are a minimum of six matching markers. Debbie, Michael, Randy, and Jorge all had between six and eight matching traits. Jackie had all twelve: a perfect match. Even for sisters, this was considered extremely rare. For us it was a sign. By this time, Dana and Jackie had been teaching together at a private Jewish school in Englewood, and they were closer than they had ever been. Jackie made her decision: she was going to donate her kidney to Dana. We all took a leave of absence, they from their school and me from mine.

At 5:00 AM, on a frigid January morning in January 2010, Steve, Jackie, Dana, and I piled into the car and drove in silence over the George Washington Bridge on our way to Columbia Presbyterian. We had gone through this routine so many times, but never did we have to say goodbye to both of our daughters at once. Dana was cracking jokes and Jackie was putting up a brave front, having watched her sister do this so many times before. I was wearing my coziest sweatpants and hoodie, but even with additional layers I could not feel warm. I did not know if I was shaking from the cold or fear. Once again, we kissed Dana goodbye as she was wheeled down the hallway. But this time, Jackie was right by her side. I kissed her goodbye and watched them be wheeled down the hallway. I was sick from seeing the fear in their eyes.

My sister, Helen, sister-in-law, Susann, brother-in-law, Michael, and Cousin Elaine were with us. I buried myself in crossword puzzle after crossword puzzle, as usual, and Steve hid behind the *New York Times*. Finally, we got word that our girls were in recovery. Steve and I flew up the stairs, no patience for elevators, to see our girls. Because of Dana's immunosuppression drugs, she was in isolation in a private room. The Nestle's Crunch bar hung from her IV pole and another was taped to Jackie's. They were both groggy but awake. Though they were in different rooms, their first words were the same: "How is my sister?"

Jackie wanted to drag herself out of bed to see Dana, while Dana demanded a wheelchair to do the same. Neither could rest until each saw the other. Finally, the following evening, we wheeled Jackie into the ICU to see Dana. They took one look at each other and burst into tears; so did we and the nurses. Jackie stood painfully to give Dana a hug; Dana, who was tethered to telemetry machines, tried to move to the edge of the bed. They looked into each other's eyes and cried, then they both broke out laughing. They had come light years from the days of intense sibling rivalry and had forged a metal bond hammered out on an anvil that could never be bent or broken.

No Good Deed Goes Unpunished

*J*ackie came home after two days, seemingly feeling well, considering she had just had an organ removed. Dana arrived home three days later. By that time, a pain had developed in Jackie's left shoulder that we erroneously attributed to sleeping "funny." But the pain increased by the day, and by the end of the week, she was readmitted to the hospital. Dana was filled with guilt.

The MRI and x-rays revealed nothing amiss, and Jackie was sent home with a prescription for oxycodone but no diagnosis. As the days went on, her pain, which was worse at night, continued to increase and the medicine did absolutely nothing to alleviate her agony. After a month of futile visits to orthopedists, Steve arranged for Jackie to be seen at Hospital for Special Surgery, renowned for orthopedics, in the hopes of obtaining a definitive diagnosis.

Dr. Shulman could not pinpoint the cause of such intense pain immediately, but she had a hunch. She had read about a syndrome that could arise from a virus or traumatic injury to the body called Parsonage-Turner Syndrome. It is, according to the Cleveland Clinic newsletter, a rare neurological disorder characterized by rapid onset of severe pain in the shoulder and arm. There were only two specialists in the country: one in Los Angeles and the other at HSS. Jackie was seen immediately. The specialist performed a test on Jackie in which he stimulated the nerves in the shoulder with an increasingly strong volt of electricity to locate the cause. It was excruciating, but it confirmed the diagnosis of this uncommon disorder. There was no treatment except physical therapy, but the doctor promised that it would eventually go away and would not leave her with permanent damage to the muscle and nerves. It took another three months, but, as promised, as suddenly as it appeared, it left.

I had taken advantage of the Family Leave Act and was home to tend to both Dana and Jackie. Even though there was pain during the recovery, we squirreled in and made the best of the situation. On a good day, the weather, with its myriad snowstorms and sleet, made it conducive to cuddling up on the couch wrapped together in fleece blankets. We watched movie after movie from Dana's supply of Disney and 80s favorites, and we laughed and sang our way through the first season of "Glee." We wanted neither visitors nor phone calls. It was a time of healing and bonding, and when old rivalries poked their heads up, this time Jackie had the upper hand.

She had given her sister a kidney, after all.

Happy Place

Jackie and Dana went back to their respective teaching jobs, and, within a year of the kidney surgery, Jackie became involved in a serious relationship with a man named Matt. He was from Westchester. They had met years ago through one of Jackie's camp friends, and dated occasionally, but now, the relationship was moving into a more serious level. Matt's parents had retired from teaching and moved from Westchester to the Berkshires, fifteen minutes from Camp Crane Lake, the sleepaway camp where Jackie had spent a glorious eleven years as a camper and counselor. That camp had provided Jackie with her closest friends and most wonderful memories. She had learned to swim and play tennis. She developed a love for gymnastics, which she carried back to Tenafly where she qualified for a local gymnastics team. She learned independence and how to navigate the world and advocate for herself. It was Jackie's Happy Place.

In February of 2012, Jackie and Matt went to his parents' house in the Berkshires for Valentine's Day weekend. They left his parents at the house, drove to her camp and walked around the deserted bunks. When they got to the lake, Matt went down on one knee in the mud and ice and proposed.

The next six months were filled with wedding plans, and,

unlike the horror stories of some, the time leading up to Jackie and Matt's wedding could not have been more joyous. Even though Matt is Christian, they decided to have a Jewish wedding. Matt proceeded to learn all he could about the rituals and customs of a Jewish wedding.

We chose the venue by the end of the month. Buying a dress became a memorable event. Jackie, Dana, Matt's mom, Rosemary, and I arrived at the dress shop. I brought plastic cups and a bottle of champagne. Jackie modeled several dresses and we all put in our two cents as to which dress had the most "wow factor." We not only left the store with Jackie's gown, but mine and Dana's as well. The guest list needed some slight tweaking and the search was on for a band. When we went for the wedding cake tasting, Jackie, Rosemary, Dana, and I drooled over the choices.

We had wanted the August ceremony to be on the venue's beautifully landscaped grounds. Since the ground was muddy from the previous night's rain, the ceremony was moved indoors to a large, airy room with floor to ceiling windows that overlooked a small lake. Swans could be seen floating back and forth. When Steve and I walked Jackie down the aisle, we felt the love of all three hundred guests in that sun-filled room. Matt stood under the chuppah, the Jewish wedding canopy, with his eyes glued on Jackie. When he stomped on the glass, the traditional ending of a Jewish wedding ceremony, all the guests, Jewish and not, yelled, "Mazel Tov!"

The reception was jubilant. It seemed everyone was on the dance floor through the entire evening. At one point, early in the evening, all joined hands to form several circles to dance the hora to Hava Nagila, the traditional song of celebration. With so many people, each circle kept crashing into the other. Guests were laughing and grabbing strangers' hands, joining a different circle going in the other direction. It was a raucous and rollicking celebration.

That August wedding was one of the happiest days of our lives. Like Dana's bat mitzvah, this wedding was not merely the union of two people in love. It was also a celebration of how far our family had come and what we had endured to get there. We celebrated the addition to our family of a young man who understood all of that and who knew the importance of his wife's previous life enough to propose to her at the very place that had helped to shape her into the woman he grew to love.

The Worst of Times, the Best of Times

Within a month of returning from their honeymoon in Aruba, Jackie was pregnant. She and Matt moved into an apartment in Mt. Kisco, a community in Westchester that provided Matt with a convenient commute into New York City for work. Jackie switched jobs and began teaching at Solomon Schechter school in White Plains, a 30-minute drive from their home. After three months of intense nausea passed, she was feeling great. Dana had finished a master's degree in library science at the University of Pittsburgh and was back in New Jersey working as a school librarian/media specialist in a local public school. The fall season went by quickly, and for the most part without incident. Steve and I appreciated the ordinariness of that time. Each of our daughters was working in jobs they liked, and we were excitedly anticipating our first grandchild.

On Valentine's Day 2013, Jackie's husband had to work. Knowing this ahead of time, I got tickets for us to see the Broadway show, "Beautiful," about the life and music of Carol King. We decided to make it into a special day for us three girls. A five-month pregnant Jackie, Dana, and I started the afternoon at the Tribeca Spa of Tranquility, where we each had a sixty-minute massage. We then lolled about in the spa's heated pool.

We left the spa feeling totally relaxed and drove uptown to the theater district, where we had a scrumptious dinner at Osteria al Doge. We were seated in a cozy nook in the upstairs balcony overlooking the noisy restaurant below. We shared a Ceasar salad followed by Penne al Pomodoro for Dana, Tagliatelle alla Bolognese for Jackie, and Pappardelle con Ragù D'Agnello for me. Any meal with Dana required something chocolate for dessert, so we shared Tortino al Choccolato. It was served with Tahitian vanilla ice cream. After dinner we strolled to the theater and enjoyed the dramatization of Carol King's life in song. At the finale, our hands burned from the extended applause that we and the rest of the audience gave the performers. It was one of the most wonderful days of my life.

Later that month, Dana began having gastrointestinal issues and difficulty digesting food. The gastroenterologist at Columbia wasn't sure of the cause, though he suspected it was Dana's gallbladder. Dana had started to lose weight and was living on crackers and pasta, the only foods she could keep down. She was feeling worse by the day; I don't know how she got out of bed, much less went to work at a demanding job.

During spring break in April, Dana spiked a fever and started vomiting profusely. Steve called Dr. Ahmed, who wanted Dana seen in the emergency room immediately. Within an hour of getting a bed in the ER, all hell broke loose. Her blood pressure plummeted, her breathing became labored, and she was intubated and put on a ventilator. Once again, we watched as she was wheeled away for emergency surgery, this time to have her gallbladder removed, once again not knowing if we would ever see her again.

A seven-months-pregnant Jackie and Matt arrived at the hospital, and we initiated Matt into our routine of keeping vigil: Steve pored over the *New York Times*, I did my crossword puzzles, Jackie leafed through People, and Matt was on his phone. In the corner of the waiting room, the television flashed pictures of the 2013 Boston Marathon. Something seemed to be happening, but since there was no sound on and we were all preoccupied, we were oblivious to the horror unfolding on the streets of Boston.

Dana came through surgery, but this time despite the removal of her gallbladder, the doctors were still not sure what had happened. She had septicemia, toxic organisms in the bloodstream, but no one knew where the infection had come from. Dr. Ahmed suspected a microscopic pinhole in her bowel, but she could not be positive. Had we not gotten her to the hospital when we did, this surely would have killed her.

Her recovery was slow and laborious. Because of the severity of the infection, her precious gift of a kidney had shut down. She was now on dialysis. We were assured by the renal doctors that although the kidney had been traumatized, the function would return as soon as it healed. Dana was discharged from the hospital and we arranged for dialysis on an out-patient basis. While she was hospitalized, she had had an extraordinarily heavy period that continued for three weeks, so in addition to being debilitated from the surgery and the infection, she was also severely anemic.

A few weeks later, Dr. Lennon, one of the renal doctors

who specialized in kidney issues, decided that Dana should have a transfusion to bring up her red blood count to treat her anemia. While in the hospital for that outpatient procedure that day, he decided to do a biopsy to check on her kidney function. I asked if the biopsy was necessary considering we were told the kidney would heal with time and also because she was already so debilitated; he assured me that it would provide valuable information. I asked him if the biopsy could cause bleeding; he dismissed my concern with scorn and condescension, claiming that the biopsy was a totally benign procedure.

The kidney biopsy took all of five minutes and as soon as he was finished, he called for the technicians to begin the blood transfusion. But before they could begin, Dana fell back onto her pillow, her face getting paler by the second. "Something's wrong," she said. I could tell immediately that Dana was bleeding internally. I had hemorrhaged when she was born and knew what loss of blood looked and felt like. I ran out into the hall and screamed for the nurse to get the doctor. By the time he came back, her blood pressure was plunging. We had to get her to the emergency room immediately. Dr. Lennon and I pushed her bed into the corridor and evacuated the first elevator that opened on our floor, but the bed was too long and couldn't fit inside. The room for out-patient procedures that Dana had been in was as far away from the emergency room as was physically possible. If it were any further, we would have been in the Hudson River. We ran to the next bank of elevators but the bed was too long for that elevator, too. Finally, we sped to the third bank of elevators and this time, the bed fit. On the first floor, we ran through the halls, knocking people out of the way, screaming for people to clear the halls, as my daughter hung like a rag doll off the side of the bed. When we finally got her to the ER, her blood pressure was 60/40. The doctors surrounded her immediately, and I was left outside of their circle.

Dana was still conscious. Once more, she stared at me with the wild eyes of a terrified horse, just like she had at the Mayo Clinic. Don't leave me, her eyes begged. The doctors wanted me out of the curtained cubicle, but I refused to leave. "She needs to see me!" I screamed. They left me alone in a corner of the small space. I believed that by sheer strength of will, I could keep Dana with us. My eyes were locked on hers, forming an invisible chain between us that kept her from floating away. It took an interminable thirty minutes to stabilize her. To this day, I wish I'd had the presence of mind to get the names of those who clearly saved her life that day. Instead, I can only remember Dr. Lennon — the arrogant man who put my daughter's life in danger.

I called Steve, and then I left a pathetic, rambling message on Matt's voicemail, afraid my panic would alarm a pregnant Jackie too much. Steve, who must have sped up the West Side Highway at ninety miles per hour, arrived at the hospital as they were wheeling her into the ICU.

Once again, we sat vigil by Dana's bed praying that her kidney was not permanently damaged by an unnecessary biopsy. Other doctors from the renal service tended to Dana, but Dr. Lennon. did not show his face for two days. Finally, he entered Dana's room waving around a paper, which held the results of the biopsy. We were impatient to hear the news and prayed that there was no permanent damage to her kidney. He proceeded to draw a picture of the kidney and began lecturing us on the workings of the organ. "We don't need a biology lesson!" Steve shouted. "Is she okay?" Dr. Lennon. hemmed and hawed, and then finally told us what we had already been told originally — that the kidney was in the process of healing itself and that with a few more weeks of dialysis, she would be fine. I thought the top of Steve's head was going to blow off. "How could you perform an unnecessary biopsy on such a debilitated patient without any backup in sight?!" Steve screamed. "Don't you dare come anywhere near my daughter! Get out of her room." Dr. Lennon. scurried out of her room, and the next visit we received from the renal service was from the head of the department.

Dana gradually regained her strength and full function of her kidney. On a warm day in June — the day Dana was going to have her dialysis port removed — Jackie went into labor.

Dylan

My first grandson was born on June 10, 2013. Matt's parents, Steve, Dana, and I sat in the waiting room anticipating the news of his arrival. I paced up and down the hospital's corridor. To say that our grandson's arrival was greeted with ecstasy would be the understatement of the year. Certainly, most babies are greeted with elation and joyful tears, but the contrast of having spent the previous two months at death's doorstep juxtaposed against the reality of the birth of this precious, red-headed baby boy heightened our bliss. Seeing my baby girl and her husband smiling into the face of their baby boy was an experience I will treasure forever.

Early in Jackie's pregnancy, Jackie and Matt told Dana that they would like to name the baby after her. They wanted to know if she would mind. In the Jewish religion, babies are not usually named for the living, but since we are not particularly observant, this was not something that bothered anyone. Dana was thrilled and honored to have her nephew named for her. They named him Dylan.

Jackie's timing was perfect. Her maternity leave coincided with the end of the school year. Jackie did not want a baby nurse; she wanted her mommy. So, I moved into Jackie's two bedroom apartment and slept on a pullout couch for the first week of Dylan's life. I got to witness Jackie and Matt fall in love with this red-headed baby boy. Taking care of an infant is like riding a bike — once you've done it, you don't forget it. I taught Jackie how to bathe Dylan without fear and how to swaddle him for sleep.

When I was a child, my mother sang a lullaby of her creation to my sister and me until we were too old to admit to anyone. When I became a mother, I sang the same lullaby to Jackie and Dana until they were too old to admit to anyone. Now, I sang that same lullaby with Jackie to her baby. The week I spent as a baby nurse was a gift I'll always cherish.

Dana had taken a medical leave from her job after the infection, and I was off for the summer. We had the summer to be with Jackie and bask with her in the delight of this beautiful child. We each rejoiced in our new roles of parent, grandparent, and aunt. Dana and I spent every day with Jackie and Dylan. We took him for walks around Mt. Kisco's downtown, and Jackie often brought him to Tenafly. We enjoyed just sitting in the yard talking, laughing, and taking turns holding Dylan. One of our favorite activities was to take him to the Englewood Boat Basin at the foot of the Palisades, on the banks of the Hudson River. We sat at a picnic table surrounded by the sheer cliffs of the Palisades on one side and the river on the other with the New York skyline in the distance. We snacked on hot dogs or hamburgers from the area's cafe and were only chased away when the yellow jackets swarmed the nearby garbage cans, which dotted the grassy area where we sat. We must have taken hundreds of photos with our iphones that summer; it was a time filled with mutual love and bonding with this new baby.

Life Hums Along

Life for all of us hummed along, and we each fell into a gloriously boring routine of living life with predictability. I had retired from teaching in June of 2010. I was working as a literacy consultant for Bergen County Special Services at an all-girls yeshiva high school on Mondays and Tuesdays. It was the perfect retirement job; I had no papers to grade and no lesson plans to create. I babysat for Dylan on Wednesdays, and on Thursdays I ran a writing group for cancer survivors.

This group was a small offshoot of the Visible Ink writing program that had been started a few years before at Memorial Sloan Kettering Cancer Center. Any former patient at MSKCC was eligible to join. The founder, and executive director of the program is Judith Kelman. It was started to provide cancer patients and survivors with an opportunity for self-expression and an opportunity to use writing as a means of diminishing stress and augmenting creativity and overall mental health. Luckily, now that I was mostly retired, I had the time to take advantage of this writing program.

The original workshops were held at the hospital and were staffed by a published writer and a social worker who was on hand to deal with the inevitable emotions that cropped up during the sessions. Each workshop provided me with an emotional outlet for the memories I harbored from my cancer six years before. The workshops were therapeutic. We were given prompts to write about our cancer diagnoses and the accompanying emotions. Just as helpful, listening to the pieces written by other participants helped us feel less alone. After a few years, the program ended the weekly workshops, but continued the one-on-one mentorship for the participants and a yearly Visible Ink publication of patients' pieces. This was topped off by the staging of fifteen chosen pieces performed by Broadway and television actors at a gala production. Some of us who had been together in the workshops for the previous two years formed our own group. Sharon and Susan offered me the use of their New York City apartments, and since I was a writing teacher, I offered to facilitate and provide the writing prompts. We've evolved into not only a writing group but a support group, as well.. It has been going strong for over eight years.

In September, Jackie returned to her job, and Dana, still weak from her ordeal, resigned from her position as a public-school librarian. The position was very demanding and although she loved being a librarian, the job had morphed into that of a computer teacher and media specialist — something that did not interest Dana at all. This, combined with her health issues — especially of the previous six months — convinced Dana that she needed a job with less stress and more enjoyment.

She had always loved working with young children and felt at home at the Tenafly Jewish Community Center, where she had worked on and off for so many years. So when a position for a Pre-K teacher in their nursery school opened, she jumped at the chance. Unfortunately, it didn't pay sufficient wages for her to live on her own, and with all of her health complications, we felt it was best that she live at home with us rather than worrying about paying rent. She made a life for herself at the JCC and was enjoying the job and those with whom she worked. Every Thursday night, she and a group of colleagues went out to the local hotel bar and hung out for a few hours. Her closest friends from college would visit occasionally and she would drive to Boston or fly to Chicago a few times a year to see them. Work was punctuated by trips to Los Angeles to visit Aunt Susann and Uncle Michael. She also went to Broadway shows and movies with her sister, friends, or cousins. At home, on work-day evenings, Steve, Dana, and I would sit at the dinner table for hours talking and laughing about our days. We would usually listen to music, but occasionally we would have MSNBC blaring in the background and we would talk politics. Every night, Dana and Jackie would text back and forth with running commentary on the latest gossip of a high school acquaintance or criticism of a particular television show.

Life was good.

Charlotte

In September 2015, Jackie and Matt informed us that they were pregnant with their second child. Jackie had severe morning sickness, as she had with her pregnancy with Dylan, but this time, though the mornings came and went, the nausea remained. Not only was she sick all day, but the usual duration of three months for severe morning sickness passed by and she felt no relief. By May, it had gotten so bad that Jackie needed to take a medical leave for the remaining few weeks of the school year.

One night, when Jackie and Matt were at our house for dinner, Dana asked if they would allow her to be in the delivery room when the time came for Jackie to give birth. Sadly, she knew it would be highly unlikely that she would ever be able to give birth to a child, and she thought being in the room with Jackie would help her experience even a small glimpse of the miracle of childbirth. My heart ached for her. Dana's childhood dream of becoming a "mommy" had been surrendered long ago. I marveled at her ability to be so open about something so personal and painful, something that she had clearly thought about and had come to accept. Dana was prepared that they might not want to share such a private event, but even before she could even get the words fully out, Jackie and Matt said yes.

The call came at 7:00 AM on July 1st, 2015. Jackie was having contractions and was on her way to the hospital. Steve, Dana, and I piled into the car and zoomed up the Saw Mill River Parkway. Unlike when Dylan was born, we were permitted to join Jackie and Matt in the labor room. We watched television and cracked jokes. Jackie's experience of labor was nothing like mine. When my children were born, women were cautioned against having an epidural because it was thought to depress the baby's breathing. Labor for me was torture, but, thankfully, not for Jackie. She was able to chat amiably with us and text her friends. Finally, at 10:00 PM, Steve, Matt's parents, and I were ushered out of the room and Dana got to witness the birth of her niece. Jackie named her Charlotte, my mother's name, though we all call her Charley.

Jackie and Matt had moved into a house in northern Westchester. Dylan, two years older than his sister, was in nursery school. Matt's mother and I took turns babysitting for Charley during the work week. Rosemary babysat on Mondays and Tuesdays, and I sat on Wednesday. This way I was able to bond with Charley as I had with Dylan. I brought her to the park across the street and met my cousin Donna, who was babysitting for her granddaughter a few miles south of Jackie's new home, for playdates. Charley was getting blonder by the day, just like her mother. She also shared the big, blue expressive eyes of her mother and aunt, but her adorable personality was all hers.

The following two years were Dana's happiest. She showered her niece and nephew with gifts. She would bring bags of books to her "munchkin" and "peanut," and they would not let her leave until she had read each book to them. She gave them one Disney film after another from her vast collection of DVDs of '80s movies and favorite shows from childhood, such as the original "Sesame Street," "The Muppet Show," and "The Electric Company." She had two cats at home, Buddy and Maggie, on whom she showered affection, and was deeply involved in her community at work. But Dylan and Charley were the absolute loves of her life.

My Body over Hers

Gradually, Dana's stamina was diminishing, and her heart rate, which had been steadily climbing, was now between 120-140 beats per minute — an extraordinarily high number even for a transplant recipient, whose heart rate is typically higher than normal.

A new catheterization revealed a leaky tricuspid valve. A few years before, Dana had a pacemaker inserted to successfully deal with brachycardia, a sudden drop in her heart rate, which left her feeling faint. Dr. Ahmed conferred with Dana's electro-cardiologist. He agreed that if they could lower her heart rate with an ablation on the sinoatrial node, she would feel immensely better. The hope was that this would allow her heart to beat more regularly. It was becoming clear that slowly, this heart, which had kept her going for almost sixteen years, was nearing its expiration date. The consensus was that she would eventually need a tricuspid valve replacement. However, this procedure was incredibly risky, even for a person without all of her complications. Dr. Ahmed was adamantly opposed to it, so much so that she told us she would lay her body over Dana's to prevent the surgery from happening. Dr. Ahmed's plan was to keep Dana going with as many tweaks as needed until such time that she could be relisted for a new heart.

During the ablation that October 2016, Steve, Jackie, and I waited in our usual spot in the lounge at Columbia. The procedure was supposed to take over an hour, but just thirty minutes after she was wheeled into the procedure room, the doctor came out and told us that the ablation wouldn't help her problem, because the leaky tricuspid valve was to blame. Dana was effectively, once more, in congestive heart failure; they would have to replace the valve. We were stunned. We had become so complacent about yet another procedure. She will have this done and then she will be fine. She will have that done and then she will be fine. The cruel irony was that she was not sick enough to be on the transplant list. Dana was devastated.

We met with the surgeon at Columbia who painted a relatively rosy scenario of the tricuspid valve replacement surgery. I felt buoyed by his assessment, but Steve, a surgeon himself, was more worried about the recovery than the actual surgery. While we were still in the waiting room, Dr. Scott, a pediatric cardiologist who had treated Dana as a baby, walked by. We recognized her and reminded her of her care over thirty-five-years ago. I thought it was a good omen. The surgery was planned for the following June. I went home with the narrative that this surgery would not be easy. It would not be fun. But she would get through it as she did everything else.

Still, it was hard to ignore the sick feeling in my stomach.

40th Birthday Parties

In December of 2016, Dana turned forty. Jackie had troubling premonitions and insisted that we throw a huge party in Dana's honor. Because of the size of our family, we had not one but two parties. The first one was a surprise party at Jackie's house with first, second, and third cousins on Steve's side of the family. Thirty relatives hid their cars a few blocks away so as not to give away the surprise before Dana even entered the house. We were a little nervous about what would happen to her heart when we yelled surprise, but she was fine and overjoyed to see all the smiling faces who were squashed into Jackie's living room. Everyone was laughing and crying and jostling others to get to Dana to give her a hug.

Two weeks later, aunts, uncles, and Dana's first cousins from my side of the family and some of Dana's old friends and colleagues from work and college gathered at Trattoria Dell'Arte, Dana's favorite restaurant on 57th street in New York City. It was within an easy walk of the Rockefeller Christmas tree and the holiday windows lining Fifth Avenue. This restaurant, directly across the street from Carnegie Hall, had been a staple of ours since it opened in the mid 1980s. It is designed like an Italian artist's studio with sculptures and drawings on the walls along with a gallery of sculpted noses of famous Italians. This was where we had celebrated Dana's December birthday for the past twenty-five years.

I met with Andrea Roman, the banquet manager, to plan the party. I explained that this was not an ordinary birthday party and gave her the background of Dana's medical difficulties. We talked for hours. Andrea was dealing with the serious illness of a dear friend, and based on that and other shared values, we formed an instant bond. She helped me plan the menu and the configuration of the room so that the atmosphere could be more open and casual than merely sitting at a long table in a restaurant. Instead of providing us with one of the banquet rooms downstairs, she did not book the other room adjacent to ours for that evening. We were able to have an open bar with room to mingle.

The night of the party, the room was aglow with hundreds of candles and torches. There was not one electric bulb in sight. Even the bar was surrounded by candles, and the effect was as if we had stepped back in time to a more romantic and elegant world. The aroma of the candles blended with the savory smells of the cacio e pepe, lasagna bolognese, chicken parmigiana, and other delectable dishes. In addition to a choice of every dessert on the menu, Andrea surprised us with a champagne toast. Dana sat regally at the head of the table, her beautiful smile exaggerated by her signature red lipstick. She soaked up the accolades of family members who toasted her. Steve, Jackie, and I each held up our glasses and spoke of our love for our birthday girl. When I think back to that lovely night, the image is bathed in candlelight.

Full Circle

Jackie's happy place was camp, but Dana's was Los Angeles. In February 2017, Dana traveled to Los Angeles on one of her many visits with Aunt Susann and Uncle Michael. She spent one of the days with her cousin, Sheri, at Disneyland, where she somehow had the energy to make it onto all the rides on her list. She spent a few weeks' worth of paychecks on gifts for Dylan and Charley, which she shipped home. Susann showered her with trips to Rodeo Drive and scheduled them for massages at an exclusive spa.

When she came home, Dana finished out the school year and prepared for the upcoming tricuspid valve surgery. As the date for the surgery grew closer, I marveled at Dana's fortitude. She had to be terrified. She would have had every right to be testy, but she wasn't. She never asked, "Why me?" I never heard her blame others. She woke up with a smile and went to bed with a smile. She had tickets with friends to see Billy Joel in late May at Madison Square Garden and had been accepted into a program for Early Childhood Certification for September. She had absorbed the lesson from so long ago: do your homework. Prepare for the future.

My writing group met every first Thursday of the month alternating at Susan's or Sharon's apartments in Manhattan. In early

May, I stepped onto the elevator at Susan's apartment building on York Avenue and saw a familiar, elderly woman standing across from me. I had not seen Dana's first pediatric cardiologist in almost thirty years, but there she was. "Dr. Kenert?" I asked. "Yes?" she said, her voice lilting up. She did not recognize me. I got off on her floor and introduced myself. "I'm Dana Tunick's mom." Even after so many years, she remembered Dana immediately. I filled her in on the latest medical news and told her that, with all that had gone on, Dana had managed to graduate from college and earn two master's degrees, one in education and one in library science. She was amazed that the little girl with the serious congenital heart defect had done so well. I hugged her goodbye and texted Dana and Steve. We all thought it was a good omen. Things were coming full circle.

The following Sunday was Mother's Day. The family gathered at my niece Robin's house. My other nieces, Kim and Debbie were also there with their children. It was a glorious, sunny day with temperatures in the low seventies. It was a bit too cool to swim in Robin's pool, but we brought the food outside and everyone sat around, soaking up the sun. Dana joked with her cousins and talked openly about the upcoming surgery, but she looked pale and could not warm herself up. While we basked in the warmth from the sun, she sat outside in her maroon puffy winter jacket and shivered.

Charley, now almost two years old, was running around the yard. We took turns keeping our eyes peeled on Charley so she didn't wind up in the pool. Dylan, now five years old, played with his cousins.

The holiday was lovely, and we were all together.

Clap for Tinker Bell

I am seven years old. The black and white images of Mary Martin as Peter Pan flicker on my living room television. Peter is just learning that Tinker Bell has accidentally swallowed poison to save Peter's life. She is dying. Her light is quivering and getting fainter. Tink flashes her weakening light and communicates to Peter that if the children in the audience believe in fairies, she will live. Desperately, Peter pleads with the audience to clap for Tinker Bell. "Oh Please! Clap for Tinker Bell! Wherever you are, if you believe, clap your hands." Sitting on the green carpet in my living room, two feet from the round picture tube, I clap wildly. I want frantically for them to hear me. It was a real emergency to me, as real an emergency as if someone had had a heart attack on my living room floor. I clap my hands until they are red and burning. Finally, Peter sees Tinker Bell's light getting brighter. "She's getting better," Peter screams. I feel an immense relief wash over me. I just helped save Tinker Bell.

Forty years later, at the Mayo Clinic, when Dana was admitted for her very first major surgery, the powerful emotions of saving Tinker Bell so long ago flooded back to me. I was a bit more mature by then, but subconsciously, the blinking light of magical thinking lived on in me. I believed that if everyone we knew thought about her at the same time, those vibrations would keep her with us. All we had to do was clap.

This belief was like my own personal harmonic convergence; power harnessed from the universe specifically for my daughter. Some people might call that the power of prayer. I did not care from what source those vibes, thoughts, or prayers arrived in Rochester, Minnesota . . . just that they did. As technology became more sophisticated, we utilized it to spread the word each time Dana was hospitalized. I had my Catholic, Protestant, Jewish, Muslim, and atheist friends all doing what they could do to pull Dana through her numerous surgeries and catastrophic illnesses, and for forty years, it had worked. Our Energizer Bunny stayed with us. It made sense to me that when her time was up, Dana silently slipped silently out of our world without warning.

We had no time to clap.

It was Friday morning, May 19, 2017. I made my way down the stairs to get coffee and I noticed that the light under Dana's bedroom door was not on. That's weird, I thought. She's always up at this time. Steve went into her room to wake her up. Then it hit me: Dana never oversleeps. By the time I got there, Steve was already shouting her name and trying to rouse her. I looked at my beautiful Dana's face and saw that it was tinged with blue. She was gone, and we both knew it.

Steve futilely performed CPR. I dialed 911 and screamed into the phone that my daughter was not breathing. I don't remember much after that except that I kept screaming, "It's not real! It's not real!" But it was real. The ambulance took her to Englewood Hospital; we followed behind. I have no memory of getting in the car, and, to this day, I do not know how Steve even remembered how to drive. After all those years and all that we had endured, was this how it would end? We knew that even if she had made it through the tricuspid valve replacement, she was still looking at another heart transplant in a few years, and, statistically, second heart transplants were very difficult.

Dana's heart had finally said enough.

The official cause of death was an arrhythmia, a condition not unheard of in someone with congestive heart failure. She left this world not with a bang, but a faint whimper. She slipped out with no pre-surgical fears, no post-op worries, no intubation, and no chest pain. Instead, she slipped away peacefully; it was the calm, and painless ending that she deserved. What was there to say that had not already been said? That we loved her? That she was courageous and heroic? Of this, we were all sure she knew.

On the morning of her death, the transplant team asked us to donate her viable organs. I wondered if she actually had any left, but she did. I thought back to the family of the donor who had brought my daughter a new beginning, and I knew Dana would be happy that she was able to give the gift of sight to someone in need and that there is now someone who gazes at the world through her beautiful blue eyes.

Traffic Problems in Fort Lee

*D*ana's funeral was on a beautiful Sunday. We warned the funeral director that we were expecting a large crowd, estimating that there would be at least 100 to 150 people. But people did not stop coming through the door. Steve, Jackie, and I were unaware of what was going on, but when one room that held 150 filled up, an adjacent room was readied to hold an additional 150.

And still they came.

Dana's favorite parking attendant at the hospital came. Dr. Ahmed and Dr. Friedman came. The entire faculty of her school came. We were later told that the line to enter the funeral home snaked around the parking lot like a line in Disneyland.

There was standing room only. The young rabbi from Jackie's school officiated. My sister, Helen, spoke. Michael and Susann spoke. And finally, it was my turn.

At first, I was inclined to talk about her illnesses. And then I thought about the events that had shaped her when she was in and out of the hospital. Steve, Jackie, and Matt stood behind me as I gave my eulogy.

"Dana was a 4'10" powerhouse of courage with silky red hair, blue eyes, and those blue lips to match. She was a little bit of everything: sarcastic, funny, and feisty — a grown woman with an old woman's experiences, a little girl who still loved anything Muppets, and a teenager who loved the Beatles and Harry Potter. She did not suffer fools. She did not sweat the minutiae. She found humor in everything, from politics to farts. It was she who kept us laughing. She read voraciously, and, in the car, listened to her eclectic playlist of over 10,000 songs that she had bought with all the Amazon gift cards she had gotten from well-wishers whenever she was in the hospital. The cover photo on her Facebook page is a picture of a proud lion with the caption: I have been fighting to survive since I was a child. I am not a survivor. I am a fucking warrior!"

At the end of the service, the funeral director stood to give directions to the cemetery. In the limo, I watched as the Fort Lee Police stopped traffic to the main highway linking Fort Lee to the myriad highways away from New York City. The police were literally stopping traffic. I recalled Dana's reaction to the former governor Chris Christie's traffic scandal of a few years ago. "Time for some traffic problems in Fort Lee."

I could hear Dana laughing.

Shiva

We decided we would sit shiva, the official period of mourning, for only three days instead of the traditional seven, or "shiva" in Hebrew. It is customary for people to bring or send food or baked goods to the mourner's home. We had mountains of cookie boxes and cakes that never even made it to the table. My oldest friend, Sherry, lovingly prepared homemade food and brought it to us each day. We had platters of deli and so much other food sent by well-wishers that it caused me anxiety knowing it could not all possibly be eaten. It is customary that food from a shiva does not leave the home of the mourners, but I could hear my mother screaming in my ear, "Oh, for God's sake! All that food is going to go to waste." In the end, though, we defied the tradition. We donated much of the leftover baked goods and non-perishables to the local Tenafly Police Dept., and brought trunk loads of cookies to Columbia Presbyterian's Heart Center to all of those who had cared for Dana. We also made sure to bring one basket to Dana's favorite receptionist, Paris, who had always greeted her with a hug.

The parade of people continued from the cemetery, and for the next three days, hundreds of people came through our door. The relatives were there, of course. Our friends were there. Jackie's friends were there. For Dana, the lines of well-wishers she had fervently hoped for after her first heart surgery finally materialized: friends from elementary school, middle school, and high school, friends from college, colleagues from every school she had ever taught in, parents of her students. Even the security guards from the JCC and the doctors who had treated her came. People from every walk of her life, including her nursery-school teacher, whom we had not seen in thirty-five years! Evelyn had somehow heard through the grapevine and showed up in our living room. So many came to our home to pay their respects and tell us what an inspiration Dana had been to them.

The parent of one of her four-year-old students told us about a special bond Dana had formed with him. He also had an illness that made it necessary to take a lot of medicine with lunch and eat a limited diet. He would not eat and he would not take his medicine unless Dana sat with him. She was the only one who could get him to comply. Another colleague told us that Dana was the only person in whom she could confide, and did not know how she would go on without her. Person after person told us stories of the effects Dana had had on their lives. We marveled at the fact that we hadn't heard these tales before, but had no doubt there were probably hundreds of other stories about her just like those.

Dana had paid it forward.

Where Is She?

How do you explain the grief of losing a child or a sister? We were devastated. Like her beloved cats, we walked around the house in disbelief, thinking she would be sitting on the couch or listening for the sound of the television in her room. When someone has been such a presence in your life and then that person is suddenly gone, it is impossible to fathom the emptiness. It cannot be comprehended. My husband, daughter, and I are faced with a huge void and are left with the nagging, unanswerable question: "Where is she?" We are rational and scientific minded and mildly religious, but not enough to provide solace or answers. Our question has only two answers: nowhere or somewhere. If nowhere, then Dana is at peace and no longer suffering. But what if she is somewhere?

The idea of somewhere comes to us in many forms. We see signs of her presence in everyday coincidences and in nature. In November, when the life-giving flowers of summer have shriveled and died, a butterfly flutters around Jackie's head and lands on her shoulder. Dana? A bright, red cardinal appears and pecks at my kitchen door. Dana? On a day that was forecast to be sunny and dry, a storm roars through the tri-state area and projects a magnificent rainbow from the Battery to the George Washington Bridge. Dana? After Dana's kidney transplant, I bought Jackie and Dana identical silver kidney bean necklaces from Tiffany's. A few years later, Jackie lost hers. I bought her a new one, which she wore every single day. Years after she had married and had children, she bent down to pick up something shiny in the driveway. It was a battered, silver kidney bean. Dana?

To feel connected, we keep her phone charged and read her numerous emails, no longer from friends and family, but from the many authors she followed. Her Facebook page provides us with hundreds of loving testimonials. Her room remains untouched. We cannot yet bear to dispose of her possessions; the documentation of her life; her glasses through which she saw the world; her stuffed lion given to her by her fourth-grade teacher to help her always remain brave: Dana the Lion-hearted.

She comes to us in dreams. Within days of her death, Jackie dreamt of a healthy-looking Dana, with no scars, looking ecstatically happy. But mostly she comes to me in music. I listen to her iPod and feel her through the sound that emanates from that rectangular piece of metal. I always listen to music and cry alone in my car; the lyrics speak to me.

On one occasion, while driving to Jackie's on the Saw Mill River Parkway — which I had renamed the Trail of Tears — I asked her for a sign. "Soliloquy" from Carousel sang out from my car radio: "My little girl, pink and white as peaches and cream is she." When they were growing up, I frequently sang that to both my daughters. I tortured them with my raspy, unharmonious voice, chasing them around the kitchen while they begged me to stop singing. However, I had never paid much attention to song lyrics until Dana died. I now realize how the lyrics of love songs apply to the love of a child, not merely a romantic partner. On another solo car ride, I again audibly asked for a sign. From my radio, these words answered: "There is a somebody I'm longing to see. I hope that she turns out to be someone who'll watch over me." I had heard that song countless times before, but this was the first time I interpreted it so personally.

In addition to these "signs," other oddly coincidental events occurred. The day after Dana died, a huge package arrived addressed to her. In it were the gifts she had bought for Charley and Dylan at Disneyland when she was there three months before in February. We were sure it was a sign.

Another weird occurrence happened two weeks after Dana's funeral. One of the shows that Dana and Jackie used to watch simultaneously was "Tyler Henry: Hollywood Medium." They would watch in their own separate homes and text throughout, commenting during the program. In one text, Jackie had said to Dana, "If anything ever happens to you, send this guy to my doorstep so I can know you are okay." Jackie was living in northern Westchester at the time, in a town on the Connecticut border. Two weeks after Dana died, she saw an ad: "Tyler Henry! The Hollywood Medium coming to the Ridgefield Playhouse next Sunday." The Ridgefield Playhouse is in a tiny Connecticut town just seven miles away from Jackie. What were the odds that someone with a successful television show in Los

Angeles would be appearing at this small theater? Jackie called the box office immediately only to be told that the event was sold out. I was shocked because I had never even heard of this entertainer, nor did I believe in people who claimed to channel the dead. Jackie told her story to the receptionist and she suggested that Jackie call each day because sometimes people who have yearly subscriptions give back tickets to shows that are of no interest to them. Each day that week, Jackie called and was told there were no tickets. Finally on Saturday, the day before the show, one ticket became available in Row D. She was convinced that Dana had, indeed, sent him to her doorstep.

Three weeks after the funeral, we were invited to a memorial for Dana at the JCC nursery school. Her colleagues had wanted to do something in her memory and they decided on a balloon release. We went to the service that they conducted, and then, we joined the seventy-five members of the faculty and went to the playground where Dana used to stand guard over her beloved students. We were each handed a balloon on our way outside. All the balloons were red in memory of Dana's magnificent red hair and the red lipstick she always wore. It was a mild night in early June. The sun was setting. Devin, the head of the nursery school, clicked on her iPad and the Beatles' "Here Comes the Sun" sang out. She instructed us to make a wish and let our balloons go. With that, a huge gust of wind blew over the playground and all the balloons that had been released were forced down, unable to ascend for several minutes. The wind whipped our hair, and the balloons danced together joyfully until it finally died down just as suddenly as it had arrived. Only then did the balloons make their way skyward.

One of Dana's favorite childhood books was Mrs. Rumphius. It is a lovely book about an old woman who instructs her grand-niece and the neighborhood children to do something in life to make the world a better place. What Mrs. Rumphius does is plant lupines all over the hills and dales of her little town for all to enjoy. My friend, Sherry, an avid gardener, told me she was planting something special in her garden in memory of Dana. Although they come in many colors, Sherry chose lupines only for their vibrant red, knowing nothing else about this flower. "Lupines," I said. "Those are the flowers in one of Dana's favorite books."

All these examples are coincidences that could be explained away, not quite enough to convince the most ardent skeptic and least spiritual person that there is more after death. I was one of those skeptics. So was my husband. Maybe it is the desperate desire to be able to connect and to believe that we will be together again that opened us up to the possibility of something else.

After Dana died, we were not the only ones in our house who were grieving. Dana's cat Maggie roamed the house in search of Dana, and Buddy was withdrawn and melancholy. One night, when I was particularly sad, he jumped into my lap and stared into my eyes. Cats do not usually hold a stare for very long, but Buddy kept my gaze and his eyes welled up with tears. I have had cats for over fifty years, and I have never seen a cat do that. A month after Dana was gone, Buddy started urinating outside of the litter box. This behavior usually indicates a urinary infection. A visit to the vet revealed no infection, however, and Dr. Glennon believed that cats grieve, and that this behavior was his way of showing his sorrow. She thought that he would continue to be non-compliant with the litter box until Dana's scent was out of the house. Sadly, she was correct. Throughout the year, Buddy would use the box sometimes but not consistently. This behavior got worse as the year wore on. We tried everything that the vet and internet suggested including putting him on tranquilizers, but the house was beginning to reek and we made the agonizing decision to find new homes for both cats in the hopes that they could be adopted together.

I scoured the internet for no kill shelters but was told by each one that they were not taking adult cats at that time. I remembered that when Dana had adopted Maggie and Buddy, we had picked them up at a woman's house on a busy street. It had rectangular windows and inside the front door were fifteen kitten cages. I had no idea how Dana had arranged the adoption or through what organization, but I became obsessed with finding this woman in the hopes that she could help me place the cats. On a Friday afternoon, I told my husband I was going to drive around to try to find the house. He thought I was crazy.

I was like a woman possessed. I did not know what street the house was on, nor did I even know what town it was in. After driving aimlessly for forty-five minutes, I realized I was near one of the pet stores that advertised adoptions one Sunday a month. It was 5:55 PM and the store would be closing at 6:00. The clerk was ringing up his last customer. I asked him if he could give me a reference for someone who could help me find new homes for two adult cats. He said, "There is a woman who just stopped in to pick something up who works for C.L.A.W.S., the cat adoption organization. She might be able to help you."

I told this woman about our decision to surrender the cats, the preferred term. She asked me if I still had the paperwork for the original adoption, and I revealed that these were my daughter's cats and that she had died the previous year. I did not know that there was paperwork, much less where it would be. I mentioned that I was on a ridiculous hunt for a house on a busy street with rectangular windows and kitten cages inside. "That's my house," she said. I started to cry and so did she. When I showed her a picture of Dana, she remembered her because of her red hair.

The cats were taken back and we were promised that they would try to find them homes together. Our vet assured us that cats who do not use the litter box for behavioral reasons almost always comply when their environment is changed. She encouraged our wrenching decision to surrender both cats because, this way, Buddy and Maggie could stay together. I am totally convinced that Dana is out there somewhere watching over us and them . How else to explain a ludicrous search for a woman with no name and a mystery house with no address that led to exactly the person I was seeking? I desperately want to believe this.

I still don't know the answer to my question, but I can choose to believe that there is some uncertain something that keeps Dana's spirit fluttering near those who cherished her. I will always see her in the beauty of the changing leaves, feel her in a warm breeze, sense her in a dream, and hear her in a song.

Dana's Memorial Library

"To live on in the hearts and minds of those we leave behind, is not to die."

— Thomas Campbell 1777-1844

For the first birthday after Dana's passing, we decided to memorialize her life by releasing red balloons and posting a video on Facebook. We asked for friends and family to do the same. We enjoyed watching the many videos of people releasing balloons in Dana's memory, but we were chastised by a cousin who was more ecologically minded than we. He suggested paper lanterns instead. So, the following year, we ordered a paper lantern from Amazon in advance of the date, and filmed our attempt to light it and send the lantern aloft. Numerous attempts failed, and, luckily, before we got too far in this endeavor we realized that if we sent a burning paper lantern up in a wooded suburban yard, we could burn the town down. Dana would have howled.

We knew that we needed a more memorable and appropriate way to commemorate Dana's birthday, but what? We wanted to do something that would be meaningful to who Dana was and would keep Dana's name and memory alive. Dana's cousin Erica came up with the best solution. A month before Dana's birthday in December, we sent out emails and posted on Facebook and

Instagram for those who were interested to please send a children's book to us. I ordered stickers with the words, "In Loving Memory of Dana Tunick," and adhered a sticker into every book. Those books would be donated to Baby's Hospital, now named Morgan Stanley Children's Hospital at Columbia Presbyterian.

On Dana's birthday, December 6, 2019, we delivered 250 books to the hospital. In 2020, we donated 300 books and in 2021, it went up to 450 books. This year, we will bring 675 books to Morgan Stanley Children's Hospital at New York Presbyterian. Because of the illnesses of the children and the immunosuppression of many, the hospital does not lend the books to the patients. Instead, each child can choose a book and take it home. Therefore, by the end of the year, the books are depleted. Our book drive not only replenishes the supply but keeps Dana's name alive in the homes of, so far, over 1,675 children.

Sacred Space

It has now been almost seven years since Dana's passing. I have learned that grief is my constant companion. The intensity of the heartache of that first year has subsided, but you never get over it. Grief can travel silently for days and then make its presence known unexpectedly from a song, a television show, or an article in *People* magazine.

When Steve, Jackie, and I look back at what helped us most profoundly to cope with our loss that year, we all agree that it was our weekly meditation sessions with our instructor, Tania. When we began, none of us had been into meditating, yoga, or anything connected with new age practices. When someone brought up the topic of meditation, Steve and I looked at each other knowingly and laughed remembering the scene in the Woody Allen movie, "Annie Hall," when Jeff Goldblum's character calls his therapist and says, "I forgot my mantra." This movie clip always made us wary of the seriousness of meditation. After all, we were also skeptical of anyone claiming to be a medium. We had thought that those claiming to bring messages from the Great Beyond were grifters who excelled at reading the subtle facial expressions of those who were gullible and frantic for proof of an afterlife. But after Dana died, I was desperate for something — anything — that would bring serenity.

One cold day in December, seven months after Dana's funeral, I googled "meditation near me." As I walked up the stairs to Sacred Space, the studio closest to my home, my intention was merely to get information. Tania opened the door and welcomed me into a peaceful cocoon of warmth and acceptance. I explained that my daughter had passed away recently and that I was searching for something to ease the pain of her loss. She enveloped me in her arms and invited me to stay for a session that was beginning in ten minutes.

Seven or eight people trickled in. Tania instructed us to get comfortable on the large pillows that dotted the floor. A chanting of Buddhist monks intoned softly in the background. I closed my eyes and Tania's gentle guidance brought me through an hour of one of the most intense experiences of my life. I felt myself floating through what looked like the pictures of the universe that I had seen in my students' science books. I imagined the brightly colored galaxies swirling through the heavens. Dana was flying with me looking healthy and serene. I felt her presence viscerally. The tears flowed copiously.

When Tania instructed us to open our eyes I was brought back to the reality of the room. The woman sitting next to me introduced herself and said, "This is going to sound weird, but I am very sensitive and open to visions." I had never laid eyes on her before that afternoon. She continued, "There was a young woman with red hair who was standing behind you with her hands on your shoulders." I gasped. I did not need more proof that Sacred Space was the place that would help me and my family heal. Jackie and I convinced my very cynical husband to join us and we embarked on a year or more of feeling the presence of Dana when we meditated. We sensed her with us at other random times, as well, but we always felt a closeness to her during our meditation sessions. We would compare notes and would inevitably find that we each "saw" similar images of Dana flying with the stars and planets, and that we all felt her presence.

It made it easier for us to let go little by little. It also gave us reassurance, not proof necessarily, but a belief in the possibility that perhaps there is more after we die. As Tania would say, "Accept the possibility. What do you have to lose?" That tranquility and new way of thinking allowed us to move forward with our grief, not to leave it behind but to carry it with us as the price one pays for love. Meditation was the vehicle that allowed us to continue with our lives and bring back the joy that we shared together as a family. We were able to laugh again and reminisce about the foibles and quirks in each of us, and loved bringing back funny stories that we knew would've had Dana doubled over in laughter. At first, the laughter was bittersweet, but, then, as time went on we laughed with full abandon. "Oh My God! Dana would have died laughing," someone would say and then, we would laugh even harder.

The pandemic put a stop to our in-person meditation. Jackie and I continued with Zoom for a while, but Steve said he had gotten from the practice of meditation what he needed.

I have gone back to practicing mindfulness meditation

lately. However, I no longer see the universe, and the vividness of Dana's spirit has diminished, though not disappeared. I am hoping she is too busy off somewhere flying through the galaxies with her grandparents and her many beloved cats from throughout her life.

Epilogue

What makes life meaningful even in the face of death? As I look back over Dana's life, I realize that that question was always below the surface of my consciousness. Steve's and Jackie's, too. Hovering over our lives with Dana was the constant shadow of death.

Who is to say what makes a life meaningful? When my father-in-law was in a nursing home in the final stages of his life, we visited one Sunday morning and found him in the dayroom participating in the Catholic mass. At this point in his mental decline, he did not always know who we were and often called his daughter, Randy, by his wife's name. So, it was no surprise that he would not remember that he was Jewish.

On reflection, noticing that he tapped his toe to the hymns and songs, it occurred to me that, perhaps, this service brought him back to a happier, early time in his life. Maybe he had lived near a church in his Bronx neighborhood and on warm days, with windows open, he recalled hearing these same tunes while doing homework at the kitchen table or while playing stickball in the streets. Maybe the music of the Mass sparked pleasurable memories in his otherwise confused and foggy mind. Did those memories give his life meaning in those final days? Who is to judge?

When I pore over our numerous photo albums and thousands of photos once the iPhone became part of our lives, I see, year after year, a happy, smiling Dana. This memoir focuses on illnesses and difficulties. But it leaves out most of the vacations and holidays, her trips to the Bahamas and London with the chorus and drama club in high school. It does not focus on the numerous plays Dana performed in from "The Music Man," "My Fair Lady," and "Antigone" in High School to being a member of the Oxford Street Players in college, which performed a different Shakespearean play each year. There is little mention of the fact that Dana made the costumes for those plays with her sewing skills that she honed during the four wonderful years that she attended Camp Buck's Rock. This memoir does not dwell on the friendships she developed with her co-workers and numerous first and second cousins nor of the enriching relationships that she maintained with her college and camp friends.

Most importantly, though it hints, it does not explore the intensely close relationship that she forged with Jackie over time. They became each other's best friend. When Jackie got engaged, it would have been understandable had Dana been jealous. Instead, she sprung into action and helped Jackie with every aspect of planning the wedding. Dana became a doting aunt to Dylan and Charley and did whatever she could to help Jackie with the kids.

I often recall the kindergarten conference with Jackie's teacher, Mrs. Saydah, when she thought Jackie had seemed withdrawn. She pulled her on her lap and asked her if everything was okay. Jackie had replied that she was worried about her sister. That worry, I believe, was part of the glue that bonded them together, and, perhaps, was the silver lining of Dana's illness.

Years ago, when we drove Jackie to Muhlenberg University for a college admissions interview, Steve and I were unexpectedly called into her meeting. The admissions counselor told us that she had asked Jackie why she was involved in a community service club at her high school for which Jackie was president in her senior year. They organized activities and workshops for children in the Paterson, NJ schools, a nearby district that lacked many amenities. The counselor told us that she always asks this question expecting the same answer," I want to help humanity, blah, blah, blah . . ." But Jackie said instead, "I was never able to do anything to help my sister, so it felt good to be able to give back to someone else." The counselor was in tears.

If I could ask Dana now if her life, with all its pain and suffering, was worth living, I would hope that she would say yes, that the scale tipped in favor of all that was loving, memorable, and enriching in her life, and that all the negative only enabled her to appreciate and cherish the positive. She loved and was loved in return.

Each person who knew Dana would have a different answer to the question of what made her life meaningful in the face of death. Over her forty years, she became the epitome of courage and strength, a source of unconditional love, and a confidante. People have told us that when they dealt with their own adversity, she provided a paradigm of how one should live a life. Scores of people regaled us with stories of how Dana affected them. Her life-long friend, Josh sent us this after her death:

My old friend . . . it was you and I who ran through the fields of the Catskills in the summers of our youth, making memories that we would talk about for decades to come. I am blessed to have known you and been with you, especially during your best years, when your health and happiness were at a maximum. You may not have been able to join me for a swim in the lake or a game on the soccer field, but you were happy just to be there, and I was happy to be with you there, not tethered to a hospital bed, but innocent and free, and this is how I'll remember you.

My old friend . . . it was you and I in the limo, laughing and joking like two perfectly normal kids, and dancing the night away. To be your date at your junior prom was my honor. You looked so beautiful. I can only hope I provided you with even a modicum of the joy you deserved in life. It must have been tough watching all your friends and classmates with their health and carefree lives knowing yours would never be that way. I'm so sorry you never got to do some of the things you wanted to do in your short life. That night meant more to me than you'll ever know, more than just a night with a friend, but a rare glimpse into your beautiful soul, to be chosen by you as your companion on that enchanted evening, to see your true form, a dancing child in youth, this is how I'll remember you.

My old friend . . . it was you and I, curled up on the couch eating nacho cheese Doritos watching the Muppet Movie for the 500th time. Then we would talk and laugh at all the stupid people in the world and their stupid clothes and the stupid music they listened to and the stupid people they voted for, and of course, all the stupid things they complained about and what they thought constituted a "hard life." Your wisdom, compassion, and life experience bypassed them all, a woman who endured more physical and mental pain before you graduated middle school than most people do their entire lives. And you never made a peep, or used it to your advantage. If you were to make an animal of yourself, abusing the world around you out of self-pity and saying fuck it all life is unfair, I would have understood. Lord knows I have thought about it, but then I would think of you and how you inverted that inner turmoil and instead used it to help others in your situation and keep all those around you in good spirits. You got me out of bed, you lifted me up, you stopped me from feeling sorry for myself. A true superhero, the heart of a champion, and an iron will to match, and this is how I'll remember you.

And your family: to whom the terms "lifetime maximum" and "pre-existing condition" have different *meanings than everyone else. Now I get it. Now I see how you got through it all with a smile. Claire, Steve, Jackie . . . no family has sacrificed more. I can only hope to have their qualities as I raise my daughter Lydia. She always loved when you came over, I'm so sorry she will never grow to know you and call you Aunt Dana. I promise you she will know all about you, your story, your courage, your compassion, your strength, the fire in your heart, your radiant red hair, this is how I'll remember you.*

My old friend . . . my oldest friend . . . from the beginning it was you and I. Throughout my life, people who I loved like brothers and sisters would vanish without a trace, never to be heard from again, leaving me lonely and confused. But you were always there. We formed a bond that carried me through the years. Friends have come and gone but you are the one friend who has always been there. Whether we are at a Pearl Jam concert, or at a Yankees game, or singing Billy Joel songs on the bus, or hanging out in your dorm, or visiting at the hospital, or sleeping over at your house, you will always be my oldest, best friend. Rest now, you must be tired from beating the devil over and over again. Relax as John and George serenade you into eternal bliss, I'll be up there soon with a bananas foster sundae from Bischoffs and we will catch up on all the stupid, amazing things in this world.

It took Dana's death to show us that her life had had meaning far outside the circle of our family and close friends. I do not know if she ever knew, but I think she sensed that it was she who taught us how to live.

The Tunick Family Photo Album

Dana at six and a half months old, July 1977

Dana and me at Dana's 2nd birthday party,
December 1978

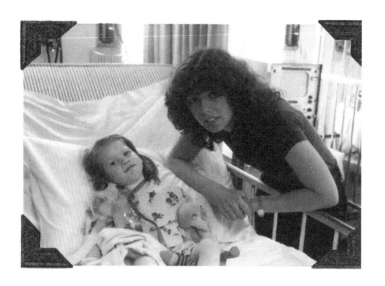

Three-and-a-half year old Dana and me at
Columbia Presbyterian, May 1979

Dana, five years old, June 1982

Jackie at
three years
old, June 1984

Dana at
Mayo Clinic,
August 1989

Dana and
Steve at Mayo
Clinic, August
1989, for
"the Fontan"
procedure

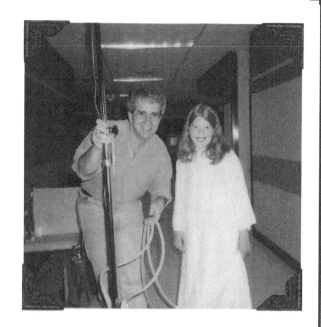

Claire, Dana,
and Jackie
at Mayo Clinic,
August 1989

Dana and
Jackie at
Mayo Clinic,
August 1989

Dana's Bat
Mitzvah,
December 1989

Jackie, Dana, and Luke Perry on the set
of "Buffy the Vampire Slayer"

Dana and Josh, Senior Prom, Spring 1995

Dana and Jackie, Crane Lake, summer 1995

Dana's graduation from Lesley College
with one of her cardiologists, May 2002

Family trip to Florida, 2002

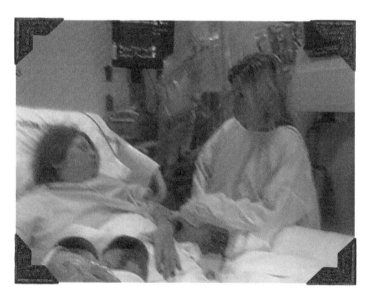

Dana and Jackie after kidney transplant,
January, 2010

Jackie and Matt's wedding, August 18, 2012

Jackie, Dana, and Claire, February 14, 2015

Dana and
Charley, 2015

Dana and
Dylan, 2016

Dana's 40th Birthday celebration,
Trattoria Dell 'Arte, December 2016

Dana, Matt, and Charley, Mother's Day May, 2017
Dana passed away five days later.

Dana's Memorial Book Drive

The entire family, 2024

Acknowledgments

This book could have never seen the light of day without the help of dear friends and writing partners. Sherry Pozner Astmann has been a friend since we were young teenagers. She was the first to read this book and went through it with a fine-tooth comb. Her discerning eye picked up missing commas and unhyphenated words. Her encouragement was essential in giving me the courage to believe this book had a life outside of my computer. Her husband, Mark Astmann, gratefully took pity on my pathetic computer skills and helped with the more technical aspects of writing, especially in formatting.

Josette Bruckman Baime was instrumental in helping me flesh out characters and events and I was buoyed by the encouragement of Daniel Baime whose opinion added to my growing confidence. Cindy Shore Goldberg, Janet Brunswick, and Elizabeth Givner read my early manuscript and provided valuable feedback that allowed me to see some of the events of this story through a more objective lens.

Lisa DiMaggio, Barbara Draimin, and Ginny Rubel, members of Blue-Sky Writers, my monthly writing group, provided vital encouragement and ways to clarify certain events in the story.

A special thank you to my sister, Helen Adrienne Spurr, who read an early version of my manuscript. Her encouragement and love have sustained me throughout my life. Annie Isen Avigdor, my college roommate, was an early reader who provided praise and support. She is also the mother of Dana's dear friend, Josh Kimmelman, who provided the moving and beautifully written reminiscence after Dana's passing.

A special thank you to Orli Zuravicky, my valued and skilled editor. She took my disjointed essays written over a period of more than twenty years and pulled them together into a coherent story that flowed smoothly along. Her suggestions to add more sensory details were invaluable in bringing clarity to my story and enhanced the reader's ability to imagine the events depicted.

My beloved daughter Jackie encouraged me to keep writing not only as a way of keeping Dana's memory alive but to provide support for other families and a narrative that life can knock you down but that it is possible to get up and thrive.

A very special thank you to my supportive and loving husband, Steve, whose critique was especially important. I know how hard it was for him to read this and relive each episode. In addition to correcting certain medical terms and events, he encouraged me to continue and see this through to fruition. I knew if he thought this story would not resonate with anyone outside of our family circle he would have told me. His opinion was crucial to how I kept writing year after year. I am forever grateful.

Claire Harris Tunick grew up and still lives in Northern New Jersey where she raised her family and taught writing and literature to middle school and high school students for over fifty years. She is recently retired and spends her time going to the gym, taking painting classes, facilitating a writing group for cancer survivors, visiting her grandchildren, and, of course, writing. She lives with her husband of fifty-four years and a stray Siamese cat who adopted them eight years ago.

Made in United States
North Haven, CT
17 January 2025

64568222R00108